Research

in

Federal Taxation

© *Copyright 1984 by*

PRENTICE-HALL, INC.
ENGLEWOOD CLIFFS, NEW JERSEY 07632

FIFTEENTH EDITION
Printed in the U.S.A.—All rights reserved

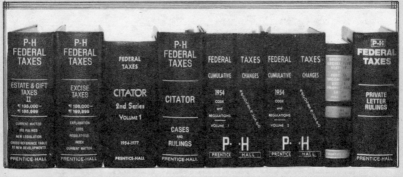

Research in Federal Taxation

With

A Complete Federal Tax Library

*The photo opposite shows a random sampling of
volumes contained in the Federal Tax Library.*

Opportunities Unlimited . . .

Today's tax professionals face the prospect of the most promising future in the history of their profession. The possibilities are great, the opportunities unlimited.

Why this unlimited opportunity? With each passing year the Federal tax laws affect American business and the individual taxpayer more and more. No businessperson, however expert in business practices, can do without a tax adviser. He or she needs help on business transactions that have tax implications, because many daily business decisions are regulated to a great degree by the tax consequences and results. And the great majority of taxpayers are becoming increasingly aware of the impact of the Federal tax on their income and personal wealth. Their investments, provisions for retirement, wills, and business-connected (or sometimes even personal) expenditures require tax planning. The tax returns of many taxpayers often get the benefit of the tax expert's care both when they are preplanned during the year, and when they are prepared before the filing due date.

The modern businessperson and professional knows that sound tax advice can save many dollars—and that poor tax advice can cost money. Therefore they must and do seek a highly qualified, properly equipped adviser who can cope with today's complicated tax laws.

To solve the problems caused by government control, the qualified adviser consults far more than the fundamentals of the Internal Revenue Code. He or she investigates and is familiar with the vast flood of regulations, rulings, cases and congressional committee reports.

Above all, in order to protect the client's interests, the practitioner must use modern working tools. By consolidating and coordinating all available information on federal taxation, the Prentice-Hall Tax Library supplies answers to the adviser's questions in a matter of minutes.

P-H FEDERAL TAXES AS A WORKING TOOL . . .

The P-H Federal Taxes Service explains the Federal tax law and all of its ramifications. The materials are arranged in 1954 Internal Revenue Code section number order. The text is amplified by examples, supported by cases and rulings, and supplemented with the full text of law and regulations and with extracts from Congressional Committee Reports explaining newly enacted laws.

EASY TO USE . . .

The system for finding information you want in P-II Federal Taxes is the simple ABC System. You need take but three steps to get complete information on any subject.

Step A—CODE SECTION NUMBER or KEY WORD APPROACH or MASTER INDEX: Select your Code section number or key words from the backbones of your Volume 2—10 binders and turn to the tab card on your subject. Backbones and tab cards show both Code section numbers and key words. Immediately after the tab card you will find a topical table of contents followed by a list of Code and Regulations sections. Either table leads you to the P-H Explanation of your topic . . . OR consult the index in Volume 1 that takes you to the Volume 2—10 location of your topic.

Step B—EXPLANATORY TEXT: Turn to the paragraph indicated in Step "A". There you will find the compilation of information on the subject.

Step C—CURRENT MATTER: Turn to the Cross Reference Tables to New Developments in Volume 11, the Current Matter Volume. Opposite the paragraph to which you are referred in Step "A", you will find paragraph references to any and all current material on your subject. Then simply refer to these paragraphs to get all the latest information.

PURPOSE OF P-H FEDERAL TAXES . . .

(1) To present the law governing Federal taxes (the Internal Revenue Code of 1954 as amended) and the regulations issued by the Commissioner of Internal Revenue interpreting it, in convenient form, up to date at all times;

(2) To classify and coordinate the rulings of the Internal Revenue Service and the decisions of the courts (many of which were rendered under prior laws) according to the law at present;

(3) To aid the subscriber and save time, by pointing out and explaining the relation between the various provisions of the Code, the purpose they are intended to accomplish, and whom they affect;

(4) To show how the law and regulations affect various situations and various classes of taxpayers, by means of explanations and examples;

(5) To provide official information even before administrative or judicial rules are made, through proposed regulations and extracts from Congressional Committee Reports explaining newly enacted law;

(6) And, above all, to organize and systematize this vast wealth of tax information so that taxpayers and their consultants can find the precedents they seek; or the most authoritative information, if no direct precedent exists.

PART I

Sources of Federal Tax Information

A FEDERAL TAX LIBRARY

Pictured on page 2 are typical volumes of a complete library of Federal Tax source information. In the complete library, you can find either the precise answer to any tax problem or authoritative information to show clearly what the answer should be. But there are over 300 books and time is your most valuable asset. How do you find *quickly and easily* the precise bit of information you want this minute?

Part II of this booklet will tell you how. Part III shows you how. You'll find the search method simple, clear, concise, complete, correct and easy-to-use, if you do one thing first; learn each set in your library as you know each club in your golf bag. That's the function of Part I of this booklet.

Source Information arises in three branches of our Federal Government, Legislative, Administrative and Judicial. In tax language, these are: (1) Congress (2) Internal Revenue Service (IRS), and (3) Courts. From these sources, it flows through law, reports, regulations, rulings and decisions into the library of volumes pictured on page 2. Single volumes are pictured on page 7.

P-H publishes the Internal Revenue Code as amended (1) and the Code as it was in any taxable year (9). Code as amended includes historical notes.

P-H publishes Regulations as amended (1) and Regulations as they were in any taxable year (9). IRS publishes its rulings in Cumulative Bulletins (C.B.'s), item (2). P-H publishes digests of IRS private rulings (11).

Court decisions are in items (3) through (6). American Federal Tax Reports (3), a P-H publication, covers all court decisions (Federal and State) on Federal tax issues. Advance sheets are in the Federal Taxes Service (7), AFTR 2d Decisions Volume. The Tax Court, formerly Board of Tax Appeals, publishes *some* decisions in item (4). P-H publishes the rest (memorandum decisions) in item (5). Advance sheets for *both* Reported and memo decisions are in item (6).

All these documents are *organized by issue* in P-H Federal Taxes, item (7). This set is both an index to the complete library and a problem-solver in itself. Flexible indexing makes issues easy to find for both a professional or occasional researcher. Volume 1 houses the tools of flexible indexing: subject, transaction, case name or ruling number. Access to law, regulation or subject is easy. Text volumes 2-10 (income tax), Estate & Gift Tax I and II, and the Excise Tax volume are all in Code Section order. Legends and section numbers on backbones and tab cards lead you to the correct division. Contents table there leads you to your issue.

The Citator, item (8), evaluates all rulings and decisions, i.e., lets you know how good they are as precedents. Congressional Committee Report extracts in your Federal Taxes Service are an invaluable aid when precedents are lacking.

Begin your research with the tax service, P-H Federal Taxes. Research steps are P-H Federal Taxes to full text volumes to Citator and supplemental aids, in that order. Before you turn to Part II, we suggest that you thumb through the rest of the pages in Part I in this booklet to gain an insight into each set in the library. Then turn to Part II for research method, problems and solutions.

Single Volumes from Federal Tax Library

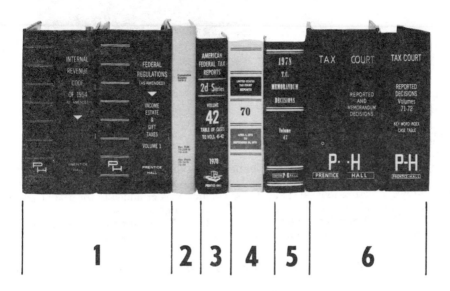

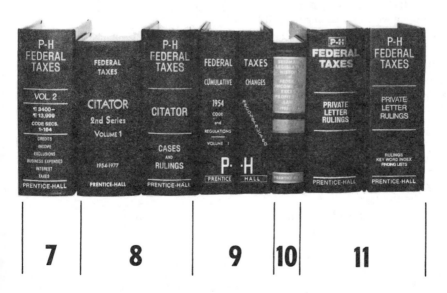

The Law
and
Regulations

The source of all federal tax law is the Internal Revenue Code and the tax regulations.

A typical section of the Internal Revenue Code is shown on page 9 *(see arrow 1)*.* In 1939 Congress codified all federal tax law into the Internal Revenue Code. Until 1954, all laws affecting federal taxes, repealed, amended or added to the 1939 Code provisions (expressly or by implication). In 1954, Congress substantially repealed the 1939 Code and enacted a new one: the Internal Revenue Code of 1954. Since then, new federal tax legislation has generally amended, added or repealed 1954 Code provisions.

NOTE: Most amendments are *express:* they change the actual language of the sections of the Code affected by the amendment. There are, however, some *implied* amendments; these refer to particular sections of the Code and change their application without changing their language. In fact, some implied amendments change the application of a Code section without referring to it all.†

The 1939 Code was amended by 15 major tax laws, and over 150 miscellaneous tax acts. The 1954 Code has been amended many times, and was substantially revised in 1958, 1964, 1969, 1976, 1978, 1981 and 1982. Congressional Committees are working on more major revisions.

Tax regulations are issued by the Treasury Department. A typical section of the tax regulations is shown opposte *(see arrow 2)**. Tax regulations are specifically authorized by law and have the force and effect of law in the taxpayer's dealings with the Treasury Department. However, a taxpayer may question the validity of a regulation in contesting a deficiency before the Tax Court or suing on a refund claim. The regulation is not controlling on the courts, but unless the courts find that the Commissioner acted in an "arbitrary or capricious" fashion (in other words, acted contrary to the *intent* of Congress), a tax regulation will stand and have the same authority as the law.

Regulations are issued and amended in the form of Treasury Decisions (T.D.'s), explained on pages 10 and 11.

---

* The Federal Government publishes the code and regulations in various forms. Illustrations are from the Prentice-Hall Code and Regulations Service. The Federal Taxes Service includes a Code Volume, and the text of Code and Regulations sections also appear next to the relevant explanations. Prentice-Hall also publishes periodically, paperbound Code and Regulations editions.

† In the Prentice-Hall Internal Revenue Code Service and the Federal Tax Service Code Volume, all amendments are referred to immediately after the text of the particular Code subsection inolved; see arrow 1a, page 9. This is not true of Government prints of the Code.

Sections from the Internal Revenue Code and Regulations

1
→

25,034 *(I.R.C.)* 8-20-81

Part II—Tax on Corporations

SEC. 11. TAX IMPOSED.

(a) Corporations in General.—A tax is hereby imposed for each taxable year on the taxable income of every corporation.

Last amendment.—Sec. 11(a) appears above as amended by Sec. 301(a) of P.L. 95-600, Nov. 6, 1978, effective (Sec. 301(c) of P.L. 95-600) for taxable years beginning after Dec. 31, 1978.

Prior amendment.—Sec. 11(a) was previously amended by Sec. 121 of Public Law 88-272, Feb. 26, 1964, effective (Sec. 131 of Public Law 88-272, Feb. 26, 1964) for taxable years beginning after Dec. 31, 1963. Sec. 11(a) as so amended is in P-H Cumulative Changes.

(b) Amount of Tax.—The amount of the tax imposed by subsection (a) shall be the sum of —

(1) 15 percent (16 percent for taxable years beginning in 1982) of so much of the taxable income as does not exceed $25,000;

(2) 18 percent (19 percent for taxable years beginning in 1982) of so much of the taxable income as exceeds $25,000 but does not exceed $50,000;

(3) 30 percent of so much of the taxable income as exceeds $50,000 but does not exceed $75,000;

(4) 40 percent of so much of the taxable income as exceeds $75,000 but does not exceed $100,000; plus

(5) 46 percent of so much of the taxable income as exceeds $100,000.

a
→

Last amendment.—Sec. 11(b) appears above as amended by Sec. 231(a)(1), (2) of Public Law 97-34, Aug. 13, 1981, effective (Sec. 231(c) of P.L. 97-34) for taxable years beginning after Dec. 31, 1981.

Prior amendments.—Sec. 11(b) was previously amended by the following:

Sec. 301(a) of P.L. 95-600, Nov. 6, 1978, effective (Sec. 301(c) of P.L. 95-600) for taxable years beginning after Dec. 31, 1978.*

Sec. 201(1) of Public Law 95-30, May 23, 1977. *

Sec. 901(a) of Public Law 94-455, Oct. 4, 1976, effective (Sec. 901(d) of P.L. 94-455) on Dec. 23, 1975.*

Sec. 4(a) of Public Law 94-164, Dec. 23, 1975. *

Sec. 303(a) of Public Law 94-12, Mar. 29, 1975, effective (Sec. 305(b)(1) of Public Law 94-12, Mar. 29, 1975) for taxable years ending after Dec. 31, 1974.*

Sec. 121 of Public Law 88-272, Feb. 26, 1964, effec-

tive (Sec. 131 of Public Law 88-272, Feb. 26, 1964) for taxable years beginning after Dec. 31, 1963.*

Sec. 2 of Pub. Law 88-52, June 29, 1963. *

Sec. 2 of Pub. Law 87-508, June 28, 1962. *

Sec. 2 of Pub. Law 87-72, June 30, 1961. *

Sec. 201 of Pub. Law 86-564, June 30, 1960. *

Sec. 2 of Pub. Law 86-75, June 30, 1959. *

Sec. 2 of Pub. Law 85-475, June 30, 1958. *

Sec. 2 of Pub. Law 85-12, Mar. 29, 1957. *

Sec. 2 of Pub. Law 458, Mar. 29, 1956. *

Sec. 2 of Pub. Law 18, Mar. 30, 1955. *

Implied amendment of Sec. 11(b) by Sec. 303(c)(1) of Public Law 94-12, Mar. 29, 1975, effective (Sec. 305(b)(1) of P.L. 94-12) for taxable years ending after Dec. 31, 1974, ceases to apply for taxable years ending after Dec. 31, 1975.

*Sec. 11(b) as so amended is in P-H Cumulative Changes.

2
→

NORMAL TAXES AND SURTAXES
DETERMINATION OF TAX LIABILITY
TAX ON INDIVIDUALS

§1.1-1 Income tax on individuals. (TD 6161, filed 2-3-56; republished in TD 6500, filed 11-25-60; amended by TD 7117 filed 5-24-71; TD 7332, filed 12-20-74.)

(a) **General rule.** (1) Section 1 of the Code imposes an income tax on the income of every individual who is a citizen or resi- ter 1 of the Code. In general, the tax is payable upon the basis of returns rendered by persons liable therefor (subchapter A, sections 6001 and following), chapter 61 of the Code) or at the source of the income by withholding. For the computation of tax in the case of a joint return of a husband

Cumulative Bulletins

The Internal Revenue Bulletin is the authoritative publication announcing the Commissioner's rulings and procedures. These are consolidated semi-annually into Cumulative Bulletin (CB) volumes pictured above. The series began in 1919 with volume 1, and continued through 30 Roman numeral volumes. Now they're identified by the year, i.e., 1981-1 and 1981-2 for the calendar year 1981. Occasionally an additional volume is issued to publish full texts of Congressional Committee Reports on newly enacted law, e.g. CB 1978-3 Volumes 1—2 for the Revenue Act of 1978 and the Energy Tax Act of 1978.

TREASURY DECISIONS—T.D.'s

On page 11 is a Treasury Decision ("T.D.") as it appears in the Cumulative Bulletin. (See arrow 1.) T.D. 7526 appears on page 451 of the 1978 Cumulative Bulletin, in the volume for the first six months of 1978. It would be cited "1978-1 CB 451." The meaning of the citation: "1978" is the year; "-1" is the first volume for that year: "C.B." is Cumulative Bulletin; and "451" is the page on which the T.D. *starts*. [*Note:* T.D. 7526 promulgated a regulation and should be cited only for that purpose. *Example:* "The regulations as promulgated by T.D. 7526, 1978-1 CB 451, etc."]

The Regulations are codified in the Code of Federal Regulations. "26 CFR" means Title 26, Internal Revenue Code of 1954 Code of Federal Regulations. TD 7526 *(Arrow 1, page 11)* has amended 26 CFR (Part 1) to add new Regulation §1.451-7. *(Arrows 2a and 2b on page 11)*. The Regulation number 1.451-7 *(Arrow 3, page 11)* starts with the prefix "1", denoting that it is an income tax regulation, followed by a decimal point. Then comes the number of the Code Section and subsection that it interprets—i.e. 451. The text of the amended or added Regulations in the Cumulative Bulletin *(Arrow 3)* is preceded by an introductory statement.

The bottom of page 11 shows how the Regulation appears in the Federal Taxes Service. The Regulation is identified as Reg. §1.451-7, and the number of the Treasury Decision that promulgated it (and later, those that amend it) are also indicated *(Arrow 4, page 11)*. In the IRS Services, Regulations are identified by the Regulation numbers (§1.451-7) without indication of the TD number. Regulations should be cited: "1954 Code Reg. §1.451-7". Then they are identifiable as codified or as published in IRS pamphlets.

A Typical Treasury Decision (T.D.)

revenue derived from the second purchase and not the first because the retailer has no obligation to redeem until the second purchase of its product.

Accordingly, because the redemption of X's *in pack* and *on pack* coupons is conditional on future purchases, they are not redeemable in cash, merchandise or other property for purposes of section 1.451-4 of the regulations and the method of accounting described in section 1.451-4 is not available with respect to its *in pack* and *on pack* coupon expenses.

---

26 CFR 1.451-6: Election to include crop insurance proceeds in gross income in the taxable year following the taxable year of destruction or damage. (Also Section 1.451-7.)

1

T.D. 7526

TITLE 26.—INTERNAL REVENUE.—CHAPTER I, SUBCHAPTER A, PART 1.—INCOME TAX; TAXABLE YEARS BEGINNING AFTER DECEMBER 31, 1953

Livestock sold on account of drought

AGENCY: Internal Revenue Service, Treasury.

ACTION: Final regulations.

SUMMARY: This document contains final regulations relating to the year in which amounts received from the sale of livestock on account of drought are included in income. Changes in the applicable tax law were made by the Tax Reform Act of 1976 [Pub. L. 94-455, 1976-3 C.B. 1, 376, 409]. The regulations provide farmers with the guidance needed to

4

FOR FURTHER INFORMATION CONTACT: David Jacobson of the Legislation and Regulations Division, Office of the Chief Counsel, Internal Revenue Service, 1111 Constitution Avenue, N.W., Washington, D.C. 20224 (Attention: CC:LR:T) (202-566-3923), not a toll-free call.

SUPPLEMENTARY INFORMATION

BACKGROUND

On Tuesday, September 20, 1977, the Federal Register published proposed amendments to the Income Tax Regulations (26 CFR Part 1) under section 451 of the Internal Revenue Code of 1954 (42 FR 47221). A correction notice was published in the Federal Register for Monday, October 3, 1977 (42 FR 53637). The amendments were proposed to conform the regulations to sections 2102 and 2141 of the Tax Reform Act of 1976 (90 Stat. 1900 and 1933). No requests for a public hearing were received and accordingly none was held. After consideration of all comments regarding the notice of proposed rulemaking, the proposed amendments as corrected are adopted by this Treasury decision.

RESPONSE TO PUBLIC COMMENTS

One public comment was received. That comment recommended that the regulations be adopted as proposed.

DRAFTING INFORMATION

The principal author of these regulations was David Jacobson of the Legislation and Regulations Division of the Office of Chief Counsel, Internal Revenue Service. However, per-

amendments to the regulations, as corrected, are hereby adopted.

The amendments to 26 CFR Part 1 and Part 7 are as follows:

Paragraph 1. Section 1.451 is deleted.

§ 1.451 [Deleted]

Par. 2. Section 1.451-6 is amended by adding the following immediately after the last sentence in paragraph (a)(1):

§ 1.451-6 Election to include crop insurance proceeds in gross income in the taxable year following the taxable year of destruction or damage.

(a) *In general.* (1) * * * For the purposes of this section, payments received under the Agricultural Act of 1949 as amended, as the result of (i) destruction or damage to crops caused by drought, flood, or any other natural disaster or (ii) the inability to plant crops because of such a natural disaster, shall be treated as insurance proceeds received as a result of destruction or damage to crops. The preceding sentence shall apply to payments which are received by the taxpayer after December 31, 1973.

* * * * *

Par. 3. A new § 1.451-7 is added immediately following § 1.451-6. The new section reads as follows:

§ 1.451-7 Election relating to livestock sold on account of drought.

(a) *In general.* Section 451(e) provides that for taxable years beginning after December 31, 1975, a taxpayer whose principal trade or business is farming (within the meaning of

2a

2b

3

[¶20,304.15] **Reg. §1.451-7** **Election relating to livestock sold on account of drought.** (TD 7526, filed 12-23-77.)

(a) **In general.** Section 451(e) provides that for taxable years beginning after December 31, 1975, a taxpayer whose principal trade or business is farming (within the meaning of §6420(c)(3)) and who reports taxable income on the cash receipts and disbursements method of accounting may elect to defer for one year a certain portion of income. The income which may be deferred is the amount of gain realized during the taxable year from the sale or exchange of that number of livestock sold or exchanged solely on account of a drought which caused an area to be designated as elibigle for assistance by the Federal Government (regardless whether the designation is made by the President or by an agency or department of the Federal Government). That number is equal to the excess of the number of livestock sold or exchanged over the number which would have been sold or exchanged had the taxpayer followed its usual business practices in the absence of

T.D.'s are drafted by the Internal Revenue Service but must be approved by the Secretary of the Treasury. With few exceptions, they promulgate new regulations or amend or repeal existing regulations. A T.D. *must* be followed by the Internal Revenue Service. This is not necessarily true of other types of rulings, as you will see on the following pages. A T.D. ranks above all other rulings appearing in the Cumulative Bulletin, since, as a regulation, it has the force and effect of law.

T.D.'s are released to the public on the day they are filed with the Federal Register—usually within a day or two after issuance and several weeks prior to their publication in the Internal Revenue Bulletin Service (issued weekly by the Government). *All* T.D.'s are publicly released.

Usually, the text of a proposed T.D., known as a "proposed regulation" is made public in tentative form before it is finally issued. The purpose is to allow at least 30 days during which interested parties may submit views, data and arguments about the proposed T.D. to the Commissioner of Internal Revenue in Washington. These must all be in writing, in duplicate. There is no set time for promulgation after expiration of the 30-day period; it may be in less than a month, or many months later, depending on the nature of the subject matter, and the volume of material submitted to the Commissioner.

In the Federal Taxes Service, all proposed amendments to income tax regulations are published in Internal Revenue Code Volume II (70,000 tab) immediately upon release. When a regulation becomes final, the proposed amendment is removed from Volume II and published, in place, at the appropriate Regulation paragraph in the text. Proposed new regulations appear in place in the compilation volumes to begin with. Each such regulation follows the Code section under which it is issued. When adopted, they are revised to reflect the final text.

All T.D.'s are published in the weekly supplements to Prentice-Hall's Federal Taxes, immediately after public release. To date, the Commissioner has issued more than 8,000 T.D.'s.

RULINGS

Revenue Rulings: Most of the rulings published by the Internal Revenue Service since 1953 have been designated Revenue Rulings (Rev. Rul.). The first Rev. Ruls. published in 1953 were numbered consecutively from 1-300. Beginning in 1954 the Rev. Rul. numbers have included the year of issuance e.g. Rev. Rul. 77-429 (1977) and Rev. Rul. 78-39 (1978).

Revenue Rulings represent the conclusions of the Internal Revenue Service on the application of the law to a given set of facts. Sometimes they are based on positions taken in rulings to taxpayers or technical advice to Service field offices. When this occurs, identifying details and confidential information are deleted to comply with statutory requirements.

Internal Revenue Bulletin (IRB and CB): The Internal Revenue Bulletin is a weekly publication of the Internal Revenue Service used by the Commissioner to announce official rulings and procedures. These Bulletins further include Treasury Decisions, Executive Orders, tax conventions, legislation, court decisions and other items of general interest.

IRS publishes in the Bulletin all substantive rulings necessary to promote a uniform application of the tax laws, including all rulings that supersede, revoke, modify or amend any rulings previously published in the Bulletin. The Bulletin is published weekly and may be obtained from the Superintendent of Documents on a subscription basis.

All rulings published in the IRB are published in the current rulings section (54,500 Tab of Volume 11) of the Federal Taxes Service at the same time that they appear in the IRB, or before in the case of advance rulings.

Rulings and procedures reported in the Bulletin do not have the force and effect of Treasury Department Regulations, but they may be used as precedents. Unpublished rulings will not be relied on, used or cited as precedents by IRS personnel in the disposition of other cases. In applying published rulings and procedures, the effect of subsequent legislation, regulations, court decisions, rulings and procedures must be considered. All published rulings apply retroactively unless otherwise indicated.

The Internal Revenue Bulletin is cited by issue number and page: e.g. IRB 1979-19, 28.

The Cumulative Bulletins (CB) are a consolidation of all items of a permanent nature published in the weekly bulletins. They are issued in two bound volumes (sometimes three) per year. The Cumulative Bulletin is cited by volume and page: e.g. 1981-1 CB 207. See also page 10.

Former ruling designations: Before 1953, IRS issued many different types of rulings. The most common were Income Tax Unit rulings (IT), Chief Counsel's Memoranda (GCM) and Published Mimeographs (Mim.). For a complete list of these rulings see the Main Table of Rulings in P-H FEDERAL TAXES, Volume 1, ¶1300.

Some of these older rulings are still in full force and effect and are cited as authority for various current rules. Many others have been declared obsolete by IRS under a review policy commenced in 1967 as announced in Rev. Proc. 67-6, 1967-1 CB 576.

Below, we illustrate how P-H FEDERAL TAXES cites rulings in the compilation *(see arrow 2)* and how full texts of rulings are published in P-H FEDERAL TAXES Current Reports *(see arrow 1).*

[¶ 54,737] RevRul 82-9, IRB 1982-2, p.5. CHARITABLE CONTRIBUTIONS AND GIFTS—What form can contributions take—gifts of appreciated property. Taxpayer donated to educational institution certain items obtained in course of drilling oil and gas wells. Items come within definition of ordinary income property in section 1.170A-4(b)(1) of the regulations. Taxpayer previously deducted costs of obtaining items as intangible drilling and development costs and has zero basis in them. Therefore, taxpayer's charitable contribution deduction is zero. Ref. ¶16,085(5). Sec. 170.

Deduction denied for ordinary income items donated from oil drilling operation to educational institution; taxpayer had previously deducted their costs as intangible drilling and development costs and has zero basis in them.

RevRul 82-9, IRB 1982-2, p. 5.

Revenue Procedures (Rev. Proc.) are published by IRS to inform the public of its internal management practices and procedures. They are published in the Internal Revenue Bulletin, and also in the Federal Register when required by the Administrative Procedure Act. Rev. Procs. began to be issued in 1955 in place of IR-Mimeographs. A typical Revenue Procedure is illustrated on page 14 at *arrow 1.*

Rev. Procs. are published in the IRB and later in the Cumulative Bulletin. Occasionally they are released in advance of publication in the IRB. Rev. Proc. 83-37, pictured at *arrow 1* page 14, was issued in advance as an Information Release. It is shown as it appeared in Federal Taxes Current Reports before its publication in the IRB.

News Release—IR.—Occasionally the Internal Revenue Service issues a News Release. These are released to the public and sometimes appear in the Cumulative

Bulletins as announcements. Generally, they remind taxpayers of obligations or benefits under new law.

Advance Revenue Procedure

1

[¶ 55,013] Adv Rev Proc 83-37 (IR-83-76). RETURNS—Time and place for filing returns—extensions of time to file—application by corporation for automatic 3-month extension. IRS announced procedure for how to apply for new six-month automatic extension of time to file corporate income tax returns. Recently issued Regs provide for six-month extension rather than previous three-month extension. Procedure applies only for tax years ending on or after 12-31-82 and before 12-1-83, because revised Form 7004, Application for Automatic Extension of Time to File Corporation Income Tax Return, will be available in 1984. Ref: ¶35,375(5). Sec. 6081.

IR-83-76. The Internal Revenue Service today [5-5-83] explained how to apply for the new six month automatic extension of time to file corporate income tax returns which is authorized by recently issued regulations.

The IRS noted that the procedure announced today applies only for tax years ending on or after Dec. 31, 1982, and

before Dec. 1, 1983, because a revised Form 7004, Application for Automatic Extension of Time to File Corporation Income Tax Return, will be available in 1984 for corporations whose tax years begin after 1982 to use when filing for automatic six months extensions.

The regulations providing for the six month extension period, rather than the previous three month extension, were published in the Federal Register on April 18, 1983. The IRS said that any three month extensions already granted will be converted to six month extensions automatically.

Revenue Procedure 83-37, is attached and will be published in Internal Revenue Bulletin No. 1983-21, dated May 23, 1983.

Adv Rev Proc 83-37

Sec. 1. Purpose

The purpose of this revenue procedure is to provide guidance to corporations that want to obtain an automatic 6 month extension of time to file Form

---

REQUESTS FOR RULINGS

Taxpayers may request rulings and determination letters and IRS personnel may seek technical advice on the tax consequences of certain transactions and the application of tax laws to specific situations.

Ruling: A written statement issued to a taxpayer or his authorized representative by the National Office (IRS headquarters) which interprets and applies the tax laws as to a specific set of facts. Rulings are issued on prospective or completed transactions before the return is filed. However, they will not ordinarily be issued if the identical issue is in a return under active examination or audit by a district office, or considered by a branch office of the Appellate Division.

Determination letter: A written statement issued by a District Director in response to a written request by an individual or an organization which applies to the particular facts of a completed transaction (affecting returns over which director has audit jurisdiction). The determination must be based on principles and precedents previously announced by the National Office (e.g., Treasury Decisions, Regulations, or rulings and other items published in the IRB).

Procedure: Requests for rulings or determination letters must meet technical requirements explained at ¶39,777 (Volume 10) of Federal Taxes. In general, each request seeking a ruling or determination letter must be signed by the taxpayer or his authorized representative. If request is signed by a representative, or if he is to appear before IRS, he must be either an attorney in good standing, a certified public accountant, or other person enrolled to practice before IRS. In each case the representative must file a written declaration that he is currently so qualified, and that he is authorized to represent his principal. A request for a ruling should be addressed to the Commissioner of Internal Revenue, Att'n: T: PS: T, Washington, D.C. 20224. A request for a determination letter should be sent to the District Director who has or will have audit jurisdiction of taxpayer's return. The request must contain a complete statement of facts relating to the transaction, including an explanation of the grounds for taxpayer's contentions and a statement of relevant authorities in support of his views.

Congressional Committee Reports

The Ways and Means Committee of the House of Representatives and the Senate Finance Committee publish reports whenever they recommend a new tax bill. If a House and Senate conference is necessary to iron out differences in proposed tax legislation, the Conference Committee issues a report.

These reports are important in interpreting tax laws, particularly new or recently amended laws. They indicate Congressional *intent* at the time a law is being enacted. Thus, before any regulations, rulings or decisions are available, you have guidance from Congress on what the law is intended to accomplish.

Committee Reports are published in P-H Federal Taxes, New Legislation tab (Volume 11). On enactment of major legislation, booklets explaining the new law are mailed to Federal Taxes subscribers. The booklets include the text of the law as amended and edited Committee Reports that explain the law as enacted. Committee Reports also appear in Federal Taxes compilation volumes until they are supplanted by Regulations on the subject. Committee Reports are later published in Cumulative Bulletins. For a comprehensive list of CB citations, see ¶7 of the How-to-Use tab in Volume 1 of the P-H Federal Taxes Service.

American Federal Tax Reports

(SECOND SERIES)   (FIRST SERIES)

The Second American Federal Tax Reports Series, cited "AFTR 2d," was begun in 1958. It streamlines federal tax case reporting, inaugurating an advance sheet system. Cases are published in P-H Federal Taxes as AFTR 2d advance sheets in the AFTR 2d Decisions Volume, as soon as they are decided. Advance sheets of each case are submitted to the judge who decided it, so he can make corrections and changes before it is reproduced in AFTR 2d bound volumes. Advance sheets are consolidated into bound volumes twice a year.

AFTR 2d uses a numbered headnote system; decisions are introduced with numbered headnotes, tied in with the P-H Federal Tax Citator. This, coupled with complete evaluation of court cases by the Citator, cuts research time to a minimum. All AFTR 2d headnotes are written by P-H tax editors.

AFTR 2d features a tie-in with P-H Federal Taxes, the key to federal tax research. Paragraph numbers assigned to cases published as advance sheets in P-H Federal Taxes are retained in AFTR 2d bound volumes. So, all of the finding aids in P-H Federal Taxes lead to full texts of decisions in AFTR 2d bound volumes. Each case in the bound volumes refers to paragraphs in P-H Federal Taxes, making a two-way tie-in.

Parallel and case tables, in the front of each volume, give official Government reporter and West National Reporter System citations. See page 18 and 19.

¶ 82-574

INLAND STEEL COMPANY, PLAINTIFF v. U.S., DEFENDANT. U.S. Court of Claims, No. 481-76, Apr. 7, 1982. Years 1964-1965. Trial Judge's opinion, 47 AFTR 2d 81-349, result adopted. Decision in part for Govt. and in part for taxpayer.

1. EMPLOYEE BENEFIT PLANS—Employer's deduction—rules applicable to plans generally—other rules. Steel co. allowed current deduction for accruals to supplemental unemployment benefit plan. Although, under union contract, some money initially spilled-over into another fund that was eventually used to finance deferred savings and vacation plan, money was returned to unemployment plan. There wasn't reasonable probability, when plan was set up, that this money would ever be used to finance deferred savings and vacation plan. *Reference:* 1982 P-H Fed. ¶19,262(50); 11,774(25). Secs. 162; 404.

2. FOREIGN INCOME—Foreign tax credit—scope and election—taxes eligible for credit—"tax denied." Corporate taxpayer wasn't allowed credit for Ontario Mining Tax (OMT) paid by its Canadian mining subsidiary; OMT didn't tax type of

Frederic W. Hickman, Lawrence M.

Dubin, Michael F. Duhl, Michael M. Conway, Hopkins & Sutter, Attys. for Plaintiff.

Robert S. Watkins, Marc Levey, Theodore D. Peyser, Donald H. Olson, Attys., John F. Murray, Act. Asst. Atty. Gen., for Defendant.

Before COWEN, Senior Judge, DAVIS and SMITH, Judges.

PER CURIAM:*

Opinion

Inland Steel Company, an integrated steel manufacturer, claimed refunds for taxes paid for calendar years 1964 and 1965 on four issues, two of which have been compromised and dismissed.[1] Two issues, the deductibility of certain accruals in Inland's Supplemental Unemployment Benefit plan (SUB) and credit for taxes paid pursuant to the Ontario Mining Tax Act (OMT), have been tried and are disposed of in this opinion, in Parts I and II respectively.

I

Supplemental Unemployment Benefit Plan—Revised Savings and Vacation Plan.

[1] This court has twice considered

The First American Federal Tax Reports Series contains Federal tax cases from the start of U.S. Federal tax laws, until the advent of the AFTR 2d Series which continues the AFTR set. Below is a page from Vol. 33, American Federal Tax Reports (First Series), cited AFTR. There are 52 volumes in this series, (1 AFTR to 52 AFTR). Here are some features of the first series:

1. *The same printing plates* used in the reporters of the West Publishing Company National Reporter System are also used in AFTR. West does not print cases in its volumes until the judge has seen proof and made all corrections The same official text used in West, appears in AFTR. When a non-tax case appears in the West volumes, it is blocked out in AFTR. Thus, condensed in a convenient set of volumes, is the *same official material* that is scattered through thousands of volumes in the West System.

2. The numbered syllabi* in West Volumes stay in AFTR. This is important in following the subsequent development of each law principle involved; see page 37. (As in the Tax Court decision on page 21, a point of law in a court decision may be strengthened or weakened by decisions, rulings, or Commissioner's act). Syllabi are also useful for quick reference in the case itself. Where the actual decision discusses the point of law digested in the syllabus, West editors insert a number at the beginning of the paragraph which matches the number of the particular syllabus.

3. AFTR page, shows full citation; *see arrows:* (1) The case appears in 65 S. Ct. 1232; (2) at 325 U.S. 365; and (3) at 33 AFTR 842.

In addition to all federal tax cases reported in the West volumes, AFTR also reprints in full thousands of federal tax cases not reported in any other recognized reporter system; AFTR has all cases on federal taxation.

Page from American Federal Tax Reports (First Series) Vol. 33

1
→

| 1232 | 65 SUPREME COURT REPORTER |

2
→

325 U.S. 365

BINGHAM'S TRUST v. COMMISSIONER OF INTERNAL REVENUE.

No. 932.

Argued April 27, 1945.

Decided June 4, 1945.

1. Courts ⊂⇒383(1)
  Internal revenue ⊂⇒1601

Government's objections to deductions of trustees' legal expenses, under income tax statute authorizing deduction of ordinary and necessary expenses incurred for production of income or for management or conservation of property held for production of income, raised questions of law reviewable by Circuit Court of Appeals and Supreme Court, notwithstanding Tax

Whether applicable statutes and regulations are such as to preclude Tax Court's decision, such as one redetermining income tax deficiencies, is a question of law reviewable by federal courts. 26 U.C.S.A. Int.Rev. Code, § 1141(c)(1).

6. Internal revenue ⊂⇒1665

Although questions whether, on Tax Court's undisputed findings, trustees' legal expenses are deductible, depending on meaning of income tax statute, present clear-cut questions of law reviewable by appellate courts, decision by Tax Court is entitled to great weight. 26 U.S.C.A. Int.Rev. Code, §§ 23(a)(2), 1141(c)(1).

7. Internal revenue ⊂⇒560

Trustees' expenses in unsuccessfully contesting income tax on appreciation in value of securities turned over to legatee,

3
→

842

Syllabi are brief statements, each covering one point of law in the decision.

AMERICAN FEDERAL TAX REPORTS
CROSS-REFERENCES

In order to have the full text of all cases relating to federal taxes, a tax practitioner would require more than 66 sets of reporters—each containing over 100 volumes, and many over 200 or 300. This is in addition to the hundreds of cases reported *only* in AFTR. All of these cases are available in only about 100 volumes of American Federal Tax Reports; 52 in the First Series and the rest in the Second Series. In order to locate any case in AFTR from its citation in a reporter system, a Cross-Reference Table appears in AFTR. Excerpts from pages of these tables are illustrated on page 19.

Illustrated are examples of complete coverage:

1. References to the Supreme Court Reporter.

2. References to the Federal Supplement Reporter, one of the series of reporters published by the West Publishing Company covering Federal courts.

3. References to official state court reporters.

State court cases may involve Federal tax issues when they determine the disposition of estate assets, the priority of liens (including tax liens), or when they reform charitable trusts to meet tax requirements.

Each AFTR (Second Series) volume contains a finding list to all Cross-Reference and Case Tables in AFTR (First Series). Similar *cumulative* tables covering AFTR (Second Series) are in each volume. See pages 5-8 in each volume.

AFTR 2d PARALLEL CITATIONS TABLES SHOWING VOLUME AND PAGE OF CASE IN GOVERNMENT AND WEST REPORTERS OPPOSITE VOLUME AND PAGE OF SAME CASE IN VOLUMES OF AFTR 2d

(For cumulative tables covering AFTR, First and Second Series, see page 7)

UNITED STATES COURTS

UNITED STATES

United States Reports Vol. Page	Same Case AFTR 2d Vol. Page
425 956	... 38 76-5580
434 77	... 40 77-6128
434 528	... 41 78-698
434 914	... 40 77-5990
434 978	... 40 77-6161
435 21	... 41 78-718
435 444	... 41 78-1565
435 561	... 41 78-1142
436 238	... 42 78-5011
436 268	... 42 78-5001
437 298	... 42 78-5198
438 901	... 42 78-5817
439 180	... 42 78-6300
439 522	... 43 79-362
440 472	... 43 79-828
444 707	... 45 80-757
447 10	... 46 80-5084
447 727	... 46 80-5174
449 292	... 47 81-519
449 383	... 47 81-523
450 1	... 47 81-797
450 156	... 47 81-855
450 944	... 47 81-910
450 1301	... 47 81-953
451 504	... 47 81-1513
451 571	... 47 81-1493
452 247	... 48 81-5115
452 249	... 48 81-5115
455 16	... 49 82-491
455 252	... 49 82-802
455 305	... 49 82-1470

SUPREME COURT REPORTER

Supreme Court Reporter Vol. Page	Same Case AFTR 2d Vol. Page
98 841	... 41 78-698
98 917	... 41 78-718
98 1153	... 41 78-1565

Supreme Court Reporter

Supreme Court Reporter Vol. Page	Same Case AFTR 2d Vol. Page
99 476	... 42 78-6300
99 773	... 43 79-362
99 1304	... 43 79-828
100 874	... 45 80-757
100 1999	... 46 80-5084
100 2439	... 46 80-5174
101 549	... 47 81-519
101 677	... 47 81-523
101 836	... 47 81-797
101 1037	... 47 81-855
101 1073	... 47 81-953
101 1408	... 47 81-910
101 1895	... 47 81-1513
101 1931	... 47 81-1493
101 2288	... 48 81-5115
102 821	... 49 82-491
102 1051	... 49 82-802
102 1082	... 49 82-1470
102 2414	... 50 82-5054

FEDERAL REPORTER SECOND SERIES

Federal Reporter 2d Series Vol. Page	Same Case AFTR 2d Vol. Page
367 778	... 18 5717
435 31	... 39 77-937
451 346	... 28 71-5972
452 144	... 28 71-5843
474 1345	... 31 73-926
476 483	... 30 72-5711
500 401	... 41 78-1086
518 747	... 36 75-5749
538 315	... 37 76-978
550 1220	... 39 77-1297
551 1090	... 39 77-1216
553 231	... 41 78-934
557 426	... 40 77-5550
557 605	... 40 77-5468
558 387	... 40 77-5450

FEDERAL SUPPLEMENT

Federal Supplement Vol. Page	Same Case AFTR 2d Vol. Page
306 620	... 25 70-960
416 865	... 38 76-5285
419 1164	... 39 77-1608
420 461	... 39 77-719
428 1297	... 40 77-6329
431 424	... 40 77-5771
433 799	... 39 77-1455;
	40 77-5586
434 113	... 39 77-1433
434 212	... 49 82-512
435 31	... 39 77-937
435 1031	... 40 77-5259
436 22	... 41 78-485
436 553	... 40 77-5463
436 760	... 41 78-474
436 1215	... 41 78-529
437 5	... 40 77-5137
437 97	... 41 78-1554
437 928	... 41 78-339
438 349	... 41 78-1117
439 99	... 40 77-5616
439 308	... 40 77-5760
439 440	... 40 77-5858
439 463	... 40 77-5954
439 907	... 40 77-5447
439 917	... 40 77-5751
439 927	... 40 77-5575

STATE REPORTERS AND REPORTS

California Reporter Vol. Page	Same Case AFTR 2d Vol. Page
144 741	... 42 78-5288

New York Miscellaneous Reports Second Series Vol. Page	Same Case AFTR 2d Vol. Page
90 939	... 42 78-6397

2
1
3

Tax Court
Reported Decisions

On page 21 you see a reported decision of the Tax Court of the United States, as it appears in the bound volumes of Tax Court Decisions (formerly Board of Tax Appeals).

Reported decisions of the Tax Court are made available to you as follows:

1. The government issues a mimeographed copy when the decision is handed down; these copies are limited in quantity to certain government officials, parties to the case, the press, and publishers of loose-leaf tax services. They are not otherwise available to the general public. Prentice-Hall publishes from this mimeographed copy as follows:

   a. The official syllabus*, preceded by digests keyed to Federal Taxes compilation volumes, appears in the weekly supplements of P-H Federal Taxes (Volume 11, tab 56,500).

   b. The full text of the decision is reported in the loose-leaf P-H Tax Court Reported and Memorandum Decisions, supplemented weekly. See page 24.

2. Pamphlets containing each *month's* decisions are printed by the government and sold to the public, and in these pamphlets the decisions are for the first time given the same page numbers they will have in the bound volumes.

3. The government prints and sells to the public bound volumes (illustrated above). These volumes are the official and permanent part of the Tax Court Decisions series. The decision is then cited by the page number. The Lay case became "69 TC 421" when incorporated into Volume 69 of Tax Court decisions.

NOTE that an official syllabus* is prepared for each point of law in a Tax Court case. When more than one point is involved, each syllabus is given an identifying number. In the illustrated case, three points are involved. The numbering of each point enables you to trace the subsequent history of the point you *are interested in* without reading through the material relating to the other points in the case.

---

*   **A syllabus** is a brief statement of one of the principles of law involved in a decision. It is also called a **headnote.** Tax Court syllabi are prepared by Tax Court personnel.

A Typical Reported Tax Court Decision

designed to prevent the avoidance of the estate tax by this sort of arrangement. Lucile's waiver of her marital rights is specifically removed from the category of statutory consideration by sections 2043(b) and 2053(e). From this result it is apparent that the claim against Franklin's estate is unsupported by any consideration recognizable under the estate tax provisions. Consequently, respondent's determination of the deficiency is upheld.

Decision will be entered under Rule 155.

LYNDELL E. AND BERNICE C. LAY, PETITIONERS v. COMMISSIONER OF INTERNAL REVENUE, RESPONDENT

Docket No. 3922–76.   Filed December 12, 1977.

Held: 1. Loan fees characterized as interest, which were paid by two accrual method partnerships in the nature of a loan discount from the principal amounts of 40-year loans, must be prorated over the entire life of each loan regardless of when the fees were actually paid.

2. A 2-percent financing fee paid by both partnerships to a mortgage banking firm was for services rendered and, therefore, is not deductible as interest in 1971.

3. The reimbursement to a partner of a FNMA preliminary commitment fee paid by him represents the cost incurred in securing a loan and, similarly, is not deductible as interest in 1971.

Byron M. Eiseman, Jr., and *Lewis H. Mathis,* for the petitioners.

Michael J. O'Brien, for the respondent.

DAWSON, *Judge:* Respondent determined a deficiency in petitioners' Federal income tax for the year 1971 in the amount of $12,749.33. Petitioner-husband is a limited partner in two partnerships that each constructed and operated a section 236 housing project under the National Housing Act. At issue is whether certain financing fees paid by these two accrual method partnerships are deductible as ordinary and necessary business expenses under section 162[1] or as interest under section 163 in

---

[1] All statutory references are to the Internal Revenue Code of 1954, as amended, unless otherwise indicated.

Tax Court
Memorandum Decisions

You usually think of a memorandum decision as one that gives no facts, no reasoning, and only the barest conclusion. For example, here is a memorandum decision of the U.S. Court of Appeals:

Leo. A. DREY, Transferee and Beneficiary, Petitioner, v. COMMISSIONER OF INTERNAL REVENUE

No. 12754.

Circuit Court of Appeals, Eight Circuit.
April 4, 1945.

On Petition to Review Decision of the Tax Court of the United States.

Stanley S. Waite, Abraham Lowenhaupt, and H. M. Stolar, all of Washington, D.C., for petitioner.

Samuel O. Clark, Jr., Asst. Atty. Gen., Sewall Key, Sp. Asst. to Atty. Gen., and J. P. Wenchel, Chief Counsel, Bureau of Internal Revenue, and

Ralph F. Staubly and John W. Smith, Sp. Attys., Bureau of Internal Revenue, all of Washington, D.C., for respondent.

PER CURIAM.

Decision of the Tax Court of the United States, 2 T.C. 291, affirmed and petition to review dismissed without the taxation of costs in favor of either of the parties in this Court, on authority of decision in Mississippi Valley Trust Company and Ruth H. Watkins, Trustees and Transferees, Petitioners v. Commissioner of Internal Revenue, 8 Cir., 147 F.2d 186, pursuant to stipulation.

But in the Tax Court it is quite another story. Tax Court (formerly Board of Tax Appeals) memorandum decision is shown on page 23. Note its length and the complete discussion of the facts and law involved.

Technically, the difference between a memorandum decision and a reported decision was originally supposed to rest on whether the point of law involved had previously been passed on. In practice, this has not been followed; as many new points appear in the memorandum decisions as appear in the reported decisions. In some years more memorandum than reported decisions are appealed to the U.S. Courts of Appeals and the U.S. Supreme Court.

Memorandum decisions started in 1928. The only reporter system including every one of these decisions is the Prentice-Hall Tax Court (formerly B.T.A.) Reported and Memorandum Decisions. *This is "5" in the complete tax library illustrated on page 7.*

NOTE: Because Tax Court memorandum decisions include thousands of points of law on taxation not found in any other source material, no tax problem has been thoroughly researched until all applicable memorandum decisions, from 1928 to date, have been checked. The one point you need to win your case may be hidden in one of these old memorandum decisions.

All memorandum decisions are carried in the P-H Citator, and all citations are located the same way as are Tax Court reported decisions.

Tax Court Memorandum Decision

permarket business, and, accordingly, respondent's determination must be sustained.

To reflect the foregoing,

Decision will be entered for the respondent.

〔¶ 82,613〕 TC Memo 1982-613. JAMES J. MORRISON. J. J. MORRISON CONSULTANTS, INC. Docket Nos. 11802-78, 1518-81, 1519-81. 10-20-82. Opinion by SCOTT, *J.* Years 1974-1977. Deficiencies redetermined.

1. ADJUSTMENTS—Allocation of income and deductions—shifting of income or deductions. Income earned for consulting services by personal service corp. was reallocated between corp. and sole shareholder. Although corp. wasn't sham and assignment of income doctrine didn't apply to tax all income to sole shareholder, facts showed shareholder's salary for 2 of 4 years didn't reflect arms-length dealing. *Ref:* 1982 P-H Fed. ¶20,910(10); 7464(5). Secs. 61; 482.

2. PERSONAL HOLDING COMPANIES—Personal holding company income—income from personal service contracts. Personal service corp. was subject to undistributed personal holding co. tax. Corporate income was personal holding co. income because written agreement with major client designated sole shareholder as individual who was to perform services and provided for termination of contract if he was unable to perform. *Ref:* 1982 P-H Fed. ¶21,384(5). Sec. 543.

3. CORPORATE DISTRIBUTIONS— Dividend and dividend-type distributions— constructive dividends—payment of personal, entertainment, travel and other expenses. Personal service corp.'s expenses disallowed because of lack of substantiation were constructive dividends to sole shareholder. Payments made to children of sole shareholder claimed to have been made in return for services were unsubstantiated and unreasonable in amount. *Ref:* 1982 P-H Fed. ¶17,089(90); 11,567(15); 16,959(75). Secs. 162; 274; 301.

Official Report

Marcus Plotkin and Robert W. Siegel, for the petitioners.

James R. Rich, for the respondent.

MEMORANDUM FINDINGS OF FACT AND OPINION

SCOTT, *Judge:* Respondent determined deficiencies in income tax of petitioner James J. Morrison for the years 1974, 1975, 1976, and 1977 in the amounts of $32,202.02, $18,256.51, $31,495.16, and $2,997.34, respectively.

Respondent determined deficiencies in income tax of petitioner J. J. Morrison Consultants, Inc., for the taxable years ended April 30, 1976, and April 30, 1977, in the respective amounts of $1,562.80 and $2,206.32.

The issues presented for decision are (1) whether certain fees for consulting services received by J. J. Morrison Consultants, Inc. were income of petitioner James J. Morrison and taxable to him rather than to his wholly owned corporation under the assignment of income doctrine; (2) whether respondent properly reallocated such consulting services income from the corporation to Mr. Morrison pursuant to section 482;[1] (3) whether for its taxable years ended April 30, 1976, and April 30, 1977, the corporation was a personal holding company and therefore subject to a personal holding company tax on its undistributed personal holding company income; (4) whether certain expenditures made by J. J. Morrison Consultants, Inc., were properly deductible business expenses; and (5) whether certain amounts expended by the corporation were for the personal benefit of James J. Morrison so as to constitute distributions made by the corporation with respect to its stock under section 301.

FINDINGS OF FACT

Some of the facts have been stipulated and are found accordingly.

Petitioner James J. Morrison resided in Windsor, Ontario, Canada, at the time of the filing of his petitions herein. Petitioner filed a U.S. Nonresident Alien Income Tax Return for the years 1974, 1975, 1976, and 1977 with the Internal Revenue Service Center, Cincinnati, Ohio.

OPINION

The first issue for decision is whether certain income reported by Morrison Consultants is that of Mr. Morrison, rather than that of Morrison Consultants, under the assignment of income doctrine. At the outset, we note that respondent does not argue that Morrison Consultants is a sham and, in fact, he concedes that it is to be treated as a corporation for Federal tax purposes.

Tax Court
Reported and Memorandum
Advance Sheets

The Prentice-Hall Tax Court service brings to you every week, the most recent reported and memorandum decisions of the Tax Court. The reported decisions are sent considerably in advance of the time you can obtain them from the Government Printing Office. The memorandum decisions are not available at all except through a service such as Prentice-Hall.

The Tax Court service consists of a permanent prong binder, plus two transfer binders sent annually to house the reported and memorandum decisions. A bound volume of memorandum decisions is also sold each year for those who want to keep up their library of bound volumes. Reported decisions are available in bound volumes (two each year) from the Government Printing Office.

The decisions in the P-H Tax Court service contain the exact text of the original decisions in the Government files and contain the Tax Court's complete findings of fact. Each decision is preceded by a digest weitten by the Prentice-Hall editorial staff which gives a clear and concise description of each issue decided in the case.

Another feature of the Prentice-Hall Tax Court service is the key-word index. The digest of each decision is prefaced by key tax words and phrases which describe in standard terms the issue in the case and which correspond to the sub-division headings in the applicable section of P-H Federal Taxes. These key words are then arranged in an index with references to the cases in which the words appear. This provides the reader with an index to the cases in the volume and at the same time relates him to the complete coverage in Federal Taxes of other cases and rulings on the same subject.

PRENTICE-HALL
FEDERAL TAXES

The Complete
—Code Arranged
Tax Service

One of the chief requirements for successful legal research is completeness. The careful tax professional wants to be able to examine every case and every ruling on any issue of concern. In the preceding pages of this booklet we have seen that the Prentice-Hall library can provide the kind of completeness that is essential. Now we are going to look at a service that provides a convenient and time-efficient access to this library, Prentice-Hall Federal Taxes.

Federal Taxes brings together all pertinent information in one place. The material is divided into subjects which follow the numerical sequence of the Code. Each subdivision consists of an explanation, the text of the applicable Code section and regulations, and related cases and rulings. The cases and rulings are in digest form and are arranged by issue into numbered paragraphs and sideheads. Paragraphs usually start with explanatory comment.

The classification of the cases and rulings by issue within each Code section has permitted the development in the service of a very complete list of digests, based on the Code arrangement and fleshed out by the titles of the numbered paragraphs which were developed from the issues. This kind of editorial treatment gives to Prentice-Hall Federal Taxes a flexible indexing *tab-card method* of research which is in addition to the classical subject matter *index* approach.

Tab Card Method—Compilation binders (Volumes 2-10) show Code section numbers AND key words. You can research from either a Code approach or a Subject approach with equal ease. See page 37.

 A. *Code Section Numbers*—The backbone of each binder shows the range of Code sections treated in that Volume. The tab cards also carry Code section numbers.

 B. *Key Words*—The words on compilation binders and tab cards are key words: e.g., Income, Partnerships, etc. Words on tab cards are key words: e.g., Deductions—Business Expenses.

Right under each tab is a topical table of contents. A numerical list of Code and regulation sections in the tab follows it. See page 37. Whether you start with Code section number or topic you find your paragraph. Every paragraph reference in the Table of Contents leads you to the "P-H Explanation" paragraph for that particular topic, at which point the rules for that section are clearly set forth.

DESCRIPTION OF FEDERAL TAXES VOLUMES

Prentice-Hall Federal Taxes *(pictured below)* consists of 17 volumes: a basic set of fourteen and three optional volumes.

Volume 1 is the index volume. It contains a subject matter index, case and rulings tables, and numerous other finding aids described more fully later on in this booklet. Volumes 2—10 contain the income tax compilation and procedure and administration. Volume 11 and the AFTR 2d Decisions Advance Sheets volume are the current matter volumes. Weekly reports containing full texts of federal court cases and IRS rulings, digests of Tax Court cases, and Report Bulletin articles are filed in these volumes. Research aids for linking the current matter with the compilation are also found here. The thirteenth and fourteenth volumes are the Code (IRC) volumes. They contain the complete text of the Internal Revenue Code of 1954 (as amended). The Code here is presented in uninterrupted numerical sequence and is in addition to the Code text interspersed throughout the compilation. Volumes 15 and 16 cover Estate and Gift taxes. Volume 17 covers Excise taxes.

FEDERAL TAXES

The Cornerstone of the P-H Tax Library

The Federal Tax Citator

WHAT THE CITATOR DOES FOR YOU.

The Citator lets you measure quickly the current precedent value of a case or ruling. And it can also direct you to later cases or rulings that deal with the same legal principle in the setting of other Code sections or fact patterns.

1. The Citator gives the history of a case. It shows whether it affirmed, reversed, modified or otherwise disposed of a lower court decision, and whether it in turn was affirmed, reversed or modified by a decision of a higher court. Related and companion cases are included in the history.

2. The Citator *evaluates* all cases and rulings. It "turns up" everything that has been said about a case or ruling in later cases or rulings. It shows at a glance the attitude of later decisions and rulings, and to what extent they accepted or rejected each principle of law involved in a given case.

In short, the Citator enables you to run down any Federal Tax decision or ruling. Starting with a given case, you can find other cases that may be more important to you because they involve facts more nearly like those in your problem. Or you may locate cases that extend or limit in some way the doctrine of your case. You may even find that your case has been questioned or overruled.

How To Use the Citator.

1. *Histories.* Each cited case (shown in bold face and capital letters) is followed immediately by its judicial history, if the case has one. The history is shown by a series of letters and abbreviations: "a" for affirmed, "r" for reversed, etc. Illustrations of the more common history items follow:

Appeal by taxpayer:

> **CHES, BERNARD J. & ROSE, 1976 P-H TC Memo ¶76,387**
> App (T) 6-16-77 (USCA 4)

Appeal by government:

> **RENSSELAER POLYTECHNIC INSTITUTE, 79 TC 967,**
> **¶79.60 P-H TC**
> App (G) 5-18-83 (USCA 2)

Appeal authorized: Sometimes the initial filing of an appeal by the government is a protective preliminary move. If so, the decision whether or not to actually appeal is announced as an appeal authorized, or not authorized.

> **CAROLINA APARTMENT INVESTORS "A" v U.S., 39 AFTR2d 77-1045 (DC Calif, 2-15-77)**
> App auth (G) 1977 P-H ¶61,000
> **CENTRAL OIL CO. v. U.S., 27 AFTR2d 71-410 (DC Miss, 10-20-70)**
> App not auth (G) 1971 P-H ¶ 61,000

Appeal dismissed:

> **PERUSICH, JOSEPH E., 1970 P-H TC Memo ¶70,120**
> d—1971 P-H ¶ 61,000 (USCA 9)

Lower court affirmed or reversed:

> **HART METAL PRODUCTS CORP., 1969 P-H TC Memo ¶ 69,164**
> a—Hart Metal Products Corp. v Comm., 27 AFTR2d 71-546, 437 F2d 946 (USCA 7)
> **JOHNSON v U.S., 24 AFTR2d 69-5474, 303 F Supp 11 (DC Va, 8-6-69)**
> r—Johnson v U.S., 27 AFTR2d 71-360, 435 F2d 1257

Higher court affirming or reversing:

> **McALISTER v COHEN, 27 AFTR2d 71-562, 436 F2d 422 (USCA 4, 1-28-71)**
> sa—McAlister v Cohen, 25 AFTR2d 70-1072, 308 F Supp 517 (DC W Va)
> **PAPA v COMM., 29 AFTR 2d 72-1403, 464 F2d 150 (USCA 2, 6-13-72)**
> sr—Papa, Frank C. & Mary, 1970 P-H TC Memo ¶ 70,090

U.S. Supreme Court: Appeals to the U.S. Supreme Court are begun by the filing of a petition for a writ of certiorari either by the taxpayer or the government.

Certiorari applied for:

> **BRIGGS, CARL v COMM., 51 AFTR2d 83-367, 694 F2d 614 (USCA 9, 12-10-82)**
> Cert filed, 2-17-83 (T)

Certiorari denied:

> **CHESTERTON, A. DEVEREAU, EST. OF v U.S., 39 AFTR 2d 1640 (Ct Cl) 551 F2d 278 (3-23-77)**
> x—Chesterton, A. Devereau, Est. of v U.S. (US) 98 S Ct 123, 10-3-77 (T)

Government will not apply for certiorari:

> **OKLA. PRESS PUBLISHING CO. v U.S., 27 AFTR2d 71-656, 437 F2d 1275 (USCA 10, 2-12-71)**
> No cert (G) 1973 P-H ¶ 61,000

Certiorari granted:

> **CENTRAL ILL. PUBLIC SERVICE CO. v U.S., 38 AFTR
> 2d 76-5691, 540 F2d 300 (USCA 7, 8-17-76)**
> Cert gr, 5-2-77 (T)

Affirming Court of Appeals which had affirmed District Court.

> **RANDALL, TRUSTEE; U.S. v, 27 AFTR2d 71-930, 401 US
> 513, 91 S Ct 991, 28 LEd2d 273 (3-24-71)**
> sa—Halo Metal Products, Inc., In re, 25 AFTR2d 70-424, 419
> F2d 1068 (USCA 7)
> s—Halo Metal Products Co., Inc., In re, 23 AFTR2d 69-777,
> 302 F Supp 614 (DC Ill)

2. *Evaluation.* The Citator's evaluation feature shows you each time a given case or ruling has been mentioned in a later decision. It pinpoints the issue for which the case was cited, gives you an insight into how the citing judge feels about the case and leads you to the exact page of the opinion on which the cited case is mentioned. These points can best be illustrated by an example. Here is the case of Granat's Estate v. Comm. as it appears in part in the Citator, 2nd Series Volume 1.

> **GRANAT, EST. OF v COMM., 9 AFTR2d 601, 298 F2d 397
> (USCA 2, 1-31-62)**
> e-1—Smurra, George, 1973 P-H TC Memo 73-1112
> e-2—Foster v Comm., 21 AFTR2d 864, 391 F2d 734 (USCA 4)
> f-2—Laughlin, James J., 1965 P-H TC Memo 65-292
> e-2—Cummings, Oswill M., Jr., 1968 P-H TC Memo 68-316
> g-2—Nigra, Nicholas J., Jr. & Beverly, 1968 P-H TC Memo
> 68-1594
> f-2—Simms, Philip R. & Nettie E., 1968 P-H TC Memo
> 68-1719
> 2—Rosenberg, Richard P., 1974 P-H TC Memo 74-35
> f-2—Hill, Thomas J. & Nancy M., 1976 P-H TC Memo
> 76-1132
> e-3—Ammel, Robert L. v Moore, Robert E., 40

Pinpoints the issue: The numeral before each citing case performs the pinpointing function. There are four decided issues or syllabi in the Granat case. These are represented by four numbered headnotes which appear with the case in volume 9 AFTR 2d. The Four issues deal with:

1. Statue of Limitations
2. Fraud Penalty
3. Reconstructions of Income
4. Bad Debts

If you are interested only in the reconstruction of income issue you need only look at the last citation (the one preceded by a "3"). The pinpointing feature enables you to zero in on those cases and those parts of the cases that deal with the issue you are researching.

Show judge's estimate of cited case: The letter, or absence of one, before each citing case accomplishes the estimate. If there is no letter, it generally means there is only a casual mention of the cited case. Such cases are usually not as valuable as those in which the citing case is discussed at some length. The nature of the discussion is characterized by a letter symbol. The first citing case explained (e) the Granat case on the statute of limitations issue. The next case explained (e) the Granat case on the fraud penalty issue. The next one followed it (f), the next one explained it and the next one distinguished it (g). The last citing case explained Granat on the reconstruction of income issue.

Other symbols used for evaluating are listed in the Citator. The order of symbols runs from complete approval ("iv," on all fours) to complete rejection ("o," overruled).

Cumulative Changes for Prior Law and Regulations

Contesting a deficiency or preparing a refund claim for a prior year requires a reference to the law and regulations in effect for that year.

The Code and Regulations as they read today are a part of the tax library. (The text is in the Code Volume and explanation volumes of Federal Taxes.) To avoid the time-consuming problem of digging up past law and piecing it together, the tax specialist turns to Cumulative Changes, published by Prentice-Hall, which does all this for him or her.

How did Code Sec. 189(d) read for calendar year 1981? Use Cumulative Changes Volume 1. Turn to pages marked with section (§) numbers, i.e. §11-p. 1; §37-p.1, etc. This code section number order makes it easy to find your page §189-p. 1. Here you will find the chart pictured on page 32. Run down the subsection (d) column *(Arrow 1)*. The section was added to the Code in 1976. The first change since it was added is effective for taxable years beginning after 1981 *(Arrow 2)*. Therefore subsection (d) as it was when added in 1976 applies for the calendar year 1981. Look for the text of subsection (d), as added in 1976, following the chart *(Arrow 3)*.

How did Reg. §1.337-6 read for calendar year 1975? Use Cumulative Changes Volume 2. Regulation numbers are carried in the center of pages. Turn to §1.337-6. It appears on top of page 21,651 as it was originally. *(Arrow 1, in illustration on page 33)*. The Regulation is shown to have been amended in 1961 *(Arrow 2)*. Therefore, to read the Regulation as in effect for 1975 (before its last amendment on 3-15-76, indicated in front of its current text in Volume 3 of the Federal Taxes Service, or in the Code and Regulations Service), read the amended text *(Arrow 2)*.

§ 189—p. 1

SEC. 189. AMORTIZATION OF REAL PROPERTY CONSTRUCTION PERIOD INTEREST AND TAXES

DATES given are effective dates.   t.y.b.a. = Taxable years beginning after.

SECTION [§] NUMBERS are those of amending Act; star (*) indicates section prescribing effective date.

Subsections in heavy black boxes are in I.R.C. as last amended.

1 **Bold-face** type indicates retroactivity beyond general effective date of Act.

AMENDING ACTS	SUBSECTIONS					
	(a)	(b)	(c)	➤(d)	(e)(1)	(e)(2)—(f)
Pub. Law 94-455, 10-4-76	Added by §201(a), §201(c)* Note 1	Added by §201(a), §201(c)* Note 1	Added by §201(a), §201(c)* Note 1	Added by §201(a), §201(c)* Note 1	Added by §201(a), §201(c)* Note 1	Added by §201(a), §201(c)* Note 1
Pub. Law 95-600, 11-6-78	§701(m)(1), §701(m)(3) (A)* Notes 1 and 2					
Pub. Law 97-34, 8-13-81		§262(a), §262(c)* t.y.b.a. 12-31-81		§262(b), §262(c)* t.y.b.a. ➤12-31-81		

2

3 ## SEC. 189. AMORTIZATION OF REAL PROPERTY CONSTRUCTION PERIOD INTEREST AND TAXES

[(a) .. As added by § 201(a), Pub. Law 94-455, 10-4-76 ..]

(a) **Capitalization of Construction Period Interest and Taxes.** — Except as otherwise provided in this section or in section 266

[(d)..As added by §201(a), Pub. Law 94-455, 10-4-76..]

(d) **Certain Residential Property Excluded.**—This section shall not apply to any real property acquired, constructed, or carried if such property is not, and cannot reasonably be expected to be, held in a trade or business or in an activity conducted for profit.

21,651

§ 1.337-6

1→ ▶ **§ 1.337-6** (Original added as § 1.337-5 by **TD 6152**, approved Nov. 25, 1955 and filed Dec. 2, 1955 and republished in **TD 6500**, approved Nov. 9, 1960 and filed Nov. 25, 1960). **Information to be filed with return.—**

There must be attached to the return of the liquidating corporation, the following information:

(a) A copy of the minutes of the stockholders' meeting at which the plan of liquidation was formally adopted, including a copy of the plan of liquidation.

(b) A statement of the assets sold after the adoption of the plan of liquidation including the dates of such sales. If section 337(c)(2)(B), relating to limited nonrecognition of gain on sales by subsidiaries, is applicable, this statement must include a computation of the total gain and of the gain not recognized under this section.

(c) Information as to the date of the final liquidating distribution.

(d) A statement of the assets, if any, retained to pay liabilities and the nature of the liabilities.

2→ ▶ **§ 1.337-6** (As amended by **TD 6533**, approved Jan. 16, 1961 and filed Jan. 18, 1961). **Information to be[1] filed.—**

(a) *Cases to which section 337(a) applies. In cases to which section 337(a) applies, there* must be attached to the return of the liquidating corporation the following information:

[2]**(1)** A copy of the minutes of the stockholders' meeting at which the plan of liquidation was formally adopted, including a copy of the plan of liquidation.

[3]**(2)** A statement of the assets sold after the adoption of the plan of liquidation including the dates of such sales. If section 337(c)(2)(B), relating to limited nonrecognition of gain on sales by subsidiaries, is applicable, this statement must include a computation of the total gain and of the gain not recognized under[4] *section 337.*

[5]**(3)** Information as to the date of the final liquidating distribution.

[6]**(4)** A statement of the assets, if any, retained to pay liabilities and the nature of the liabilities.

(b) *Cases to which section 337(d) is applicable.—In cases to which section 337(d) applies, a minority shareholder who claims credit or refund of tax deemed to have been paid shall file with the return on which the claim is made (or Form 843) a statement containing the name and address of the liquidating corporation and the district in which it files its return, together with all information necessary to support the validity of his claim and a detailed computation of the amount of his claim.*

Footnote § 1.337-6 (TD 6500).—§ 1.337-6 (formerly § 1.337-5) was promulgated by TD 6152, and republished in TD 6500, without change.

Footnote § 1.337-6 (TD 6553).—Matter in *italics* added to § 1.337-6 by TD 6533, approved Jan. 16, 1961 and filed Jan. 18, 1961, which struck out:

(1) "filed with return.—There"
(2) "(a)"
(3) "(b)"
(4) "this section"
(5) "(c)"
(6) "(d)"

Seidman's Legislative History

"In no other area of the law has legislative history played such an important part." Professor Erwin C. Surrency, Journal of Taxation, August 1965. The sole or clinching argument in a tax dispute may come from an explanation of the law during its course through Congress. Seidman's Legislative Histories* make these explanations available to you.

For example, if you seek that explanation for Code Sec. 852(c), find the origin in P-H Cumulative Changes. It shows it was carried-over from 1939 Code to 1954 Code. It was amended in 1958 by Public Law 85-866. The Committee Report finding list in P-H Federal Taxes, ¶7, shows where to find, in Cumulative Bulletins, all 3 Committee Reports explaining the 1958 amendment. For earlier legislative history, turn to P-H Federal Taxes, Code (IRC) Volume II, Appendix Tables, Table II and thence to Seidman's.

1954 Code

SEC. 852. TAXATION OF REGULATED INVESTMENT COMPANIES AND THEIR SHAREHOLDERS.

*   *   *   *   *   *   *   *   *   *   *   *   *

(c) **Earnings and Profits.**—The earnings and profits of a regulated investment company for any taxable year (but not its accumulated earnings and profits) shall not be reduced by any amount which is not allowable as a deduction in computing its taxable income for such taxable year.

Appendix—Table II

1954 Code Sec. No.	1939 Code Sec. No.
852	362(a),(b)(1)-(7)

Seidman's

SEC. 362. TAX ON REGULATED INVESTMENT COMPANIES.

(a) **Earnings and Profits.**—The earnings and profits of a regulated investment company for any taxable year beginning after December 31, 1941 (but not its acmumulated earnings and profits) shall not be reduced by any amount which is not allowable as a deduction in computing its net income for such taxable year.

Committee Reports

Report—Senate Finance Committee (77th Cong., 2d Sess., S. Rept. 1631).—Under the various amendments made by your committee, the election by an investment company to be a regulated investment company will produce, among others, the following tax consequences:

1. In the determination of the earnings and profits of such a company for any taxable year beginning after December 31, 1941, such earnings and profits shall not be reduced by any amount which is not allowable as a deduction in computing its net income for such taxable year. Thus, if a corporation would have had earnings and profits of $500,000 for the taxable year 1942 except for the fact that it had a net capital loss of $100,000, which was not deductible in determining its net income for that year, its earnings and profits for 1942 if it is a regulated investment company would be $500,000. However, in determining its accumulated earnings and profits as of January 1, 1943, the earnings and profits for 1942 to be considered in such computation would amount to $400,000, assuming there had been no distribution from such earnings and profits. Due to the change made in the concept of

*There are three books by Seidman: *Legislative History of Federal Income Tax,* 1861-1938 Laws @ $30; 1939-1953 Laws, two volumes @ $30 each; *Legislative History of Federal Excess Profits Tax Laws,* 1946-1917., @ $20.

Private Letter Rulings
The Key to
IRS Private Rulings

For many years the IRS has been issuing private rulings to individual and corporate taxpayers on a wide range of specific transactions, ranging from mergers to handling of medical expenses. The law requires all private rulings requested by taxpayers after October 31, 1976 to be made public by the IRS, after deleting details identifying the taxpayer and certain other privileged information. While IRS and Congress still insist that a private letter ruling can be used as a precedent only by the taxpayer to whom it was issued, such rulings obviously show the IRS probable approach in a given situation.

The IRS estimates that about 5,000 private rulings, each about four pages long, will be released annually.

P-H Private Letter Rulings Service, a valuable addition to the tax library, is your key to this great mass of additional rulings. It publishes, in weekly reports, digests of Private Letter Rulings which the IRS issues on a weekly basis. It brings you these digests, classified according to the Code Sections that they interpret and by key words, in weekly pamphlets that you file in the binder. Weekly and cumulative indexes and rulings finding lists, permit a quick search of rulings by Key Word, Code Section, and IRS ruling number. Also, each digest includes references to pertinent paragraphs in P-H Federal Taxes where you can find related explanations, cases and rulings. Bound volumes of the year's digests include a key word index and finding lists.

Subscribers to Private Letter Rulings can obtain copies of full texts of rulings from Prentice-Hall for a small additional fee. Also, the IRS has announced that it will make the full text of private letter rulings available on a subscription basis (the subscriber must agree to take all the rulings), and that individual rulings may also be requested from it by IRS ruling number, at a higher cost.

Internal Memoranda of the IRS

The Internal Revenue Service on January 11, 1982, began to release the full text of internal IRS memoranda prepared after December 24, 1981. On April 23, 1982, IRS commenced the release of internal memoranda that were prepared between July 4, 1967 and December 24, 1981. All of these pre-December 24, 1981 memoranda will be released in reverse chronological order by December 24, 1983. The memoranda consist of: (1) General Counsel Memoranda (GCMs) prepared by the Office of Chief Counsel to the IRS in response to a formal request for legal advice from the Assistant Commissioner of·Internal Revenue, (2) Technical Memoranda (TMs) drafted by the Legislation and Regulations Division of the Office of Chief Counsel in connection with proposed Treasury decisions or regulations, and (3) Actions on Decisions (AODs) prepared in the Tax Litigation Division of the Office of Chief Counsel and directed to the Chief Counsel whenever IRS loses cases in the Tax Court, Federal District Court, Court of Claims or U.S. Court of Appeals.

We have designed *Internal Memoranda of the IRS* to enable you to quickly and easily find and retrieve the full text of these memoranda and related materials of interest to you. The Service includes all memoranda prepared after December 24, 1981. Subscribers to the Service may also order the full text of any pre-December 24, 1981 memoranda they wish.

Subscribers to the service will receive each week a Report Bulletin in pamphlet form consisting of two parts. Part I contains the full texts of the post-December 24, 1981 internal memoranda released that week by IRS arranged according to the related Code section. Each memorandum will be preceded by a brief headnote prepared by our editors. The headnote will identify by key-word the subject matter of the memorandum and the IRS document number. At the end of each headnote, you will find a reference to related paragraphs in the P-H *Federal Taxes* service. Part II of each weekly Report Bulletin contains subject matter indexes and cross-reference tables identifying the subject matter of the pre-December 24, 1981 GCMs and TMs released in the last week by IRS.

PART II

Key to Research Equipment— P-H Federal Taxes

Prentice-Hall Federal Tax Equipment is the key to source material on federal taxes. All information from sources mentioned, on a given point, is compiled into an orderly text, and is kept up to date with weekly supplements. The next 11 pages illustrate the arrangement of text and weekly supplements. Pages 40 through 43 show text material from P-H Federal Taxes. Pages 44-48 show items from the weekly supplement. Supplements keep the basic text up to date; all decisions, rulings and other interpretations are reported weekly and are tied in with the text through cross reference tables. Note these features:

1. *Pilot Chart*—¶16,500. Presents a bird's-eye view of the entire division; it points out the highlights of each subject. Pilot charts are described further on page 62.

2. *P-H Explanation*—¶16,981. Each subdivision begins with an editorial explanation. These are boxed so they are highly visible.

3. *Law Paragraph*—¶16,981.15. This is a verbatim reprint of 1954 Code Sec. 280A. Note that *italics* and footnote show you the last amendment and how the law read before the change. The vertical "law lines" uniformly identify statutory material in P-H Federal Taxes. Congressional Committee Reports follow the law, officially explaining new law, if not yet reflected in regulations.

4. *Regulation*—¶16,981.18-B. A verbatim reprint of the regulation is reproduced in the text, identified by the "Key" symbol. The symbol means that the material is an official regulation having the force and effect of law to the extent that it correctly reflects the law.

5. *Annotations paragraphs*—¶16,982 shows how the law has been applied in cases and rulings. The cases and rulings are classified by principles of law (issues), and their judicial history is supplied.

6. *Additional research aids,* covered starting with page 56.

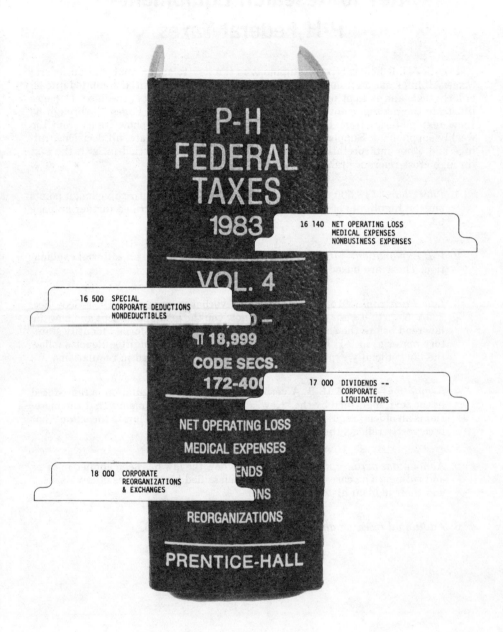

P-H
FEDERAL
TAXES
1983

VOL. 4

¶ 18,999

CODE SECS.
172-400

NET OPERATING LOSS

MEDICAL EXPENSES

REORGANIZATIONS

PRENTICE-HALL

16 140   NET OPERATING LOSS
         MEDICAL EXPENSES
         NONBUSINESS EXPENSES

16 500   SPECIAL
         CORPORATE DEDUCTIONS
         NONDEDUCTIBLES

17 000   DIVIDENDS --
         CORPORATE
         LIQUIDATIONS

18 000   CORPORATE
         REORGANIZATIONS
         & EXCHANGES

UNDER THE TAB CARD

Right under the tab is a topical table of contents. A numerical list of Code and Regulation sections follows it. Both are illustrated below. Whether you start with Code or Regulation section number or topic, you find your paragraph.

SPECIAL CORPORATE DEDUCTIONS— NONDEDUCTIBLES SPECIAL RULES

TOPICAL TABLE OF CONTENTS

◄─ C

FINDING LIST OF CODE AND REGULATION SECTIONS

A ↗

B ├──────➤

Whether you begin your research with *Code* section number (*Arrow A*), *Reg.* section number (*Arrow B*) or *topic* (*Arrow C*), it's always wise to jot down the topic reference (*Arrow C*).

HERE'S WHY:

a) You get the basic rules explained and defined.

b) Tax saving suggestions.

c) Annotations immediately follow the explanation. They are *classified by issue* and *new developments* are cross-referred to annotations paragraphs by *issue*.

	Pilot Chart	16,505

[¶16,500] ● Pilot Chart—Special Corporate Deductions—Nondeductibles—Special Rules—

SPECIAL CORPORATE DEDUC-TIONS	**Dividends received deductions.—** *General rules.*—Corporations are allowed various special deductions for dividends received. General rules for allowance of the deduction are explained in ¶16,559. *Dividends from domestic corporations.*—Subject to the restrictions and limitations mentioned in ¶16,564, corporations are allowed a deduction equal to 85% of any dividends received from taxable domestic corporations. The deduction is 100% if the recipient is a Small Business Investment Company and files a required statement to that effect. A 100% deduction is also allowed where a dividend is paid by one corporation to another in the same affiliated group. ¶16,564. *Dividends from public utilities.*—A special rule applies in computing the deduction for dividends received on the preferred stock of taxable public utilities. The recipient corporation must take into account the fact that the utility may have been allowed a partial deduction for the dividend payment in computing its own tax. ¶16,565. *Dividends from foreign corporations.*—A limited deduction is allowed for qualified dividends from foreign corporations, if the foreign corporation is taxable and, 50% or more of the foreign corporation's gross income for period of 36 months is from income effectively connected with conduct of a U.S. trade or business. However, if the dividend meets the requirements of Sec. 243(d), it may qualify for treatment as a dividend from a domestic corporation for purposes of the deduction. ¶16,566. *Exceptions, restrictions and limitations* on allowance of these deductions are explained at ¶16,567. **Dividends paid on utility preferreds.—**Public utilities are allowed a limited deduction for dividends paid on certain preferred stock, except to the extent the dividends represent current distributions of unpaid amounts accumulated in taxable years ending before October 1, 1942. ¶16,569. **Organization expenses.—**A corporation may elect to defer its organizational expenses and deduct them ratably over a period of not less than 60 months. ¶16,575.
DISALLOW-ANCE OF CERTAIN EXPENSES IN CONNECTION WITH BUSINESS USE OF HOME, RENTAL OF VACATION HOMES, ETC.	**Deductions,** by individuals, partnerships, trusts, estates, and Subchapter S corporations for home offices and rented vacation homes are sharply limited. For full explanation, see ¶16,981.

DISALLOWANCE OF CERTAIN EXPENSES IN CONNECTION WITH BUSINESS USE OF HOME, RENTAL OF VACATION HOMES, ETC.

P-H EXPLANATION

¶16,981   Deductions by individuals, partnerships, trusts, estates, and S corporations for home offices and rented vacation homes are limited. Sec. 280A, ¶16,981.15.

(a) Home office deduction.—Self-employeds and employees can't take any home office deductions unless they're allocable to a part of the home used *exclusively* and on a *regular* basis as the principal place of business

P-H EXPLANATION

for any trade or business of the taxpayer's. Formerly, only a primary business qualified. This change is retroactively applied to tax years after 1975 that aren't closed by the statute of limitations. Also the deduction is allowed if the home is used as a place for meeting or dealing with patients, clients or customers in the normal course of business, or in the case of a separate structure not physically attached to the taxpayer's house, in connection with his or her trade or business. An employee must further prove that the exclusive use is for the convenience of the employer. Sec. 280A(a), and (c)(1). Despite the home office limitation, taxpayers may still deduct interest, taxes, etc. allocable to their home work areas since these deductions don't depend on the use of the premises for a business purpose. Sec. 280A(b). See ¶16,982(5).

L [¶16,981.15]   CODE SEC. 280A.   DISALLOWANCE OF CERTAIN EXPENSES A IN CONNECTION WITH BUSINESS USE OF HOME, RENTAL OF VACA-W TION HOMES, ETC.

(a)   **General Rule.**—Except as otherwise provided in this section, in the case of a taxpayer who is an individual or an [1] *S* corporation, no deduction otherwise allowable under this chapter shall be allowed with respect to the use of a dwelling unit which is used by the taxpayer during the taxable year as a residence.

(c)   **Exceptions for Certain Business or Rental Use; Limitation on Deductions for Such Use.—**

(1)   **Certain business use.**—Subsection (a) shall not apply to any item to the extent such item is allocable to a portion of the dwelling unit which is exclusively used on a regular basis—

(A)   the principal place of business for any trade or business of the taxpayer,

(B)   as a place of business which is used by patients, clients, or customers in meeting or dealing with the taxpayer in the normal course of his trade or business, or

(C)   in the case of a separate structure which is not attached to the dwelling unit, in connection with the taxpayer's trade or business.

In the case of an employee, the preceding sentence shall apply only if the exclusive use referred to in the preceding sentence is for the convenience of his employer.

[Footnote ¶16,981.15]   Matter in *italics* in Sec. 280A(a), (e)(1) and (f)(2), added by section 5(a)(26)(A)—(B), '82 Subchapter S Revision Act which struck out:

(1)   "electing small business"

Effective date (Sec. 6, '82 Subchapter S Revision Act).—Generally applies to taxable years beginning after 12-31-82. For transitional rules and exceptions, see footnote ¶33,349.

Proposed Reg. §1.280A-1 continued
(j) **Effective date.** This section and §§1.280A-2 and 1.280A-3 apply to taxable years beginning after December 31, 1975.

☞ **Proposed Reg. §1.280A-2**

○━➤ [¶16,981.18-B] **Proposed Reg. §1.280A-2 Deductibility of expenses attributable to business use of a dwelling unit used as a residence.** (Proposed Treasury Decision, published 8-7-80; 7-21-83.)

(a) **Scope.** This section describes the business uses of a dwelling unit used as a residence for which items may be deductible under an exception to the general rule of section 280A and explains the general conditions for the deductibility of items attributable to those uses. Deductions are allowable only to the extent provided in section 280A(c)(5) and in paragraph (i) of this section. See §1.280A-1 for the general rules under section 280A.

(b) **Use as the taxpayer's principal place of business—(1) In general.** Section 280A(c)(1)(A) provides an exception to the general rule of section 280A(a) for any item to the extent that the item is allocable to a portion of the dwelling unit which is used exclusively and on a regular basis as the principal place of business for any trade or business of the taxpayer.

(2) **More than one business.** For purposes of section 280A(c)(1)(A) and this section, a taxpayer is deemed to have a principal place of business for each trade or business in which the taxpayer engages. For example, a university professor whose principal place of business for teaching is the university may use a portion of a dwelling unit as the principal place of business for the professor's retail sales business.

(3) **Determination of principal place of business.** When a taxpayer engages in a single trade or business at more than one location, it is necessary to determine the taxpayer's principal place of business for that trade or business in light of all the facts and circumstances. Among the facts and circumstances to be taken into account in making this determination are the following:
(i) The portion of the total income from the business which is attributable to activities at each location;
(ii) The amount of time spent in activities related to that business at each location; and
(iii) The facilities available to the taxpayer at each location for purposes of that business.
For example, if an outside salesperson has no office space except at home and spends a substantial amount of time on paperwork at home, the office in the home may qualify as the salesperson's principal place of business.

(c) **Use by patients, clients, or customers in meeting or dealing with the taxpayer in the normal course of business.** Section 280A(c)(1)(B) provides an exception to the general rule of section 280A for any item to the extent the item is allocable to a portion of the dwelling unit which is used exclusively and on a regular basis as a place of business in which patients, clients, or customers meet or deal with the taxpayer in the normal course of the taxpayer's business. Property is so used only if the patients, clients, or customers are physically present on the premises; conversations with the taxpayer by telephone do not constitute use of the premises by patients, clients or customers. This exception applies only if the use of the dwelling unit by patients, clients, or customers is substantial and integral to the conduct of the taxpayer's business. Occasional meetings are insufficient to make this exception applicable.

Proposed Reg. §1.280A-3(f) continued

(5) **Allocation rule.** The provisions of paragraph (c) of this section shall apply if any person with an interest in the unit is deemed to use the unit for personal purposes on any day during the taxable year. The provisions of paragraph (c) of this section shall be applied on the basis of the taxpayer's expenses for the unit, the number of days during the taxable year that the unit is rented at a fair rental (determined without regard to the provisions of §1.280A-1(g)), and the number of days during the taxable year that the unit is used for any purpose.

(6) **Limitation on deductions.** The provisions of paragraph (d) of this paragraph shall be applied on the basis of the taxpayer's rental income and expenses with respect to the unit.

CASES AND RULINGS BY ISSUE

	Paragraph [¶]		Paragraph [¶]
Cases and rulings	16,982	(6) Sale of home used for business	
(1) Retroactive law change		(8) Storage use of home	
(3) Dwelling unit defined		(10) Rental arrangements	
(5) Business use of home			

P-H EXPLANATION

¶16,982 Cases and rulings.—The rulings must be read subject to Sec. 123, P.L. 96-369, 10-1-80, Amending Acts, Code Vol., which prohibits implementing or enforcing any ruling with respect to Sec. 280A that relates to certain topics described at ¶16,981.

(1) **Retroactive law change.**—Effective for tax years beginning after 1975, expenses of home offices used exclusively and regularly as principal place of secondary business are deductible, and vacation homes aren't used for personal purposes when rented to family members at fair rental value.
IR-82-32, ¶54,852 P-H Fed. 1982.

(3) **Dwelling unit defined.**—Deduction denied for mini-motorhome used partially for personal purposes. Mini-motorhome was dwelling unit, and Sec 280A limitations applied.
Ronald L. Haberkorn, 75 TC 259.

Deduction denied taxpayer even though he lived in resort complex excepted as hotel from Sec. 280A limitations. Condominium unit was used for private purposes and not as hotel for at least 20 days: taxpayer enjoyed full right of access and possession, and owed resort complex no duty other than as unit owner.
Fine v U.S. (DC Ill;1980), 46 AFTR2d 80-5617, 493 F.Supp. 540, aff'd (7 Cir;1981), 47 AFTR2d 81-1478, 647 F2d 763.

(5) **Business use of home.**—Client initiated phone calls satisfied dealing with client requirements for home office deduction. Manager of condominiums used room exclu-

Married teachers using one room in their home exclusively and regularly for teaching-related activities can't take business expense deduction for portion of mortgage and utilities attributed to room. Room is used to prepare lessons, construct charts and learning centers, read educational literature, file materials and to store textbooks, periodicals, slides and other material. Room must be principal place of business; be used by patients, clients or customers; or be separate structure unattached to home.
LtrRul 7734023, 5-24-77, ¶55,830 P-H Fed. 1977.

Proprietor of hot dog stand couldn't deduct any part of expenses attributable to her business use of kitchen and bookkeeping room in her residence. Residence wasn't principal place of business, hot dog stand was.
Rudolph Baie, 74 TC 105.

Dermatologist's management of 6 rental properties was a second business. He could deduct expenses of office in private residence used solely in connection with rental business and cost of travel between office and rental properties. He wasn't restricted to one principal place of business.
Edwin R. Curphey, 73 TC 766 (pending 9 Cir).

Home office deductions denied as pharmacist and as secretary-treasurer of pharmacy.

MAIN CROSS REFERENCE TABLE

How to use this table effectively.—The entries below are designed to give you the last word in up-to-the minute developments. They provide the key to latest Internal Revenue Service rulings, proposed new regulations and amendments, court proceedings and recent cases. The references tie paragraphs of your Federal Taxes directly to items of current interest in your Report Bulletins.

To get the most out of your Compilation, follow this system:

1.   Start with the paragraph number of the subject you are interested in
2.   Find the number in the table below in the column headed"From ¶"
3.   Look opposite the number in the column headed "To ¶". There you will find the paragraph number of each related current item concerning you. References to AFTR2d cases (e.g. ¶82-312) will be found in the AFTR 2d Advance Sheets or in the latest bound volume of the AFTR 2d series (e.g. 47 AFTR 2d).

≫→   For latest information released after this table was printed, see the *Supplementary Cross Reference Table* beginning on page 61,501.

61,556   Main Cross Reference Table ¶ 16,958(30)–17,036   6-23-83

From ¶	To ¶	
16,958(30) .	. . . . . .	*Brill, David,* pending CA 2 (T)
	57,859	*Sciales:* Lost diary. TCMem

		Disallowance of Certain Expenses in Connection with Business Use of Home, Rental of Vacation Homes, Etc. (§280A)
16,981 . . .	60,265	Employee loses home-office deduction for room used for after-office-hours calls. Ed
16,982(5). .	. . . . . .	*Cousino, Paul W. v Comm.,* cert den 11-29-82 CA 6 (T)
	. . . . . .	*Moskovit, Leonard A.,* pending CA 10 (T)
		Warganz, Joseph F. v Comm., aff by unpublished order 10-15-82 CA 3
	56,530	*Loughlin:* Mobilehome was dwelling unit; home office of pilot. DC
	57,006	*Odom, Jr.:* Bedroom wasn't used exclusively for business. TCMem, aff by unpublished order 4-15-83 CA 4
	57,019	*Smith:* No part of home used exclusively for office. TCMem
	57,034	*Drucker:* Concert violinist's home practice room. TC, pending CA 2 (T)
	57,052	*Anderson:* Anesthetist-farm owner's home office. TCMem
	57,054	*Rogers:* Concert basoonist's home practice room. TCMem, app dis 1-21-83 CA 2 (T)
	57,055	*Cherry:* Concert cellist's home practice room. TCMem, app dis 1-21-83 CA 2 (T)
	57,056	*Dempsey:* Music practice room in home. TCMem
	57,101	*Perrote:* Research project was connected with regular job. TCMem
	57,165	*Weightman:* School located in crime ridden area. TCMem
	57,171	*Trussel:* Housing judge used home office. TCMem
	57,178	*Hauser:* Political election campaign expenses. TCMem
	57,501	*Lopkoff:* 25% of work done at home in evening. TCMem
	57,778	*Cally:* Patients use of home office wasn't shown. TCMem
	57,867	*Wilhelm:* Deduction for home office expenses denied. TCMem
	83-326	*Moller:* Home offices; managing portfolios worth $14 million. CtCl
	83-5022	*Green rev:* Room to receive clients' phone calls. CA
16,982(8). .	83-348	*Druker* aff: Atty. wasn't in business of selling products. CA, cert den 5-31-83 CA 2 (T)
16,982(10) .	57,623	*Baker:* Use while donating time; allocation of interest and taxes. TCMem
	57,884	*Gilchrist:* Nonvacation home rental; repeal of Sec. 280A. TCMem
	83-302	*Bolton* aff: Method of allocating limitation on deducting rental expenses. CA

83-5804   U.S. v. DEAK-PERERA & CO.
                          Cite as 52 AFTR 2d 83-000

The majority also observed in Calandra that the exclusionary rule's "primary purpose" is to deter future unlawful conduct by government agents, not to redress past injury to its victims, and that "[a]s with any remedial device, the application of the rule [is] restricted to those areas where its remedial objectives are ... most efficaciously served." 414 U.S. at 347-48. Assuming arguendo that a single IRS special agent possesses all the attributes of a grand jury as a "grand inquest," see Blair v. United States, 250 U.S. 273, 282 (1919), when he issues a subpoena, and that it is, indeed, the spirit of the exclusionary rule which inhibits this Court's finding of an abuse of process in the agent's use of the subpoena here, the Court remains of the opinion that to decline to enforce it will have the salutary effect of deterring calls for regulatory inspections to gain entre to an inspectee's premises on less benign errands and that its original ruling is, thus, consistent with Calandra.

For the foregoing reasons, therefore, it is, this 17th day of August, 1983,

Ordered, that petitioner's motion for reconsideration is denied.

¶ 83-5223

Ernest DRUCKER, Patricia Rogers, Philip Cherry and Ruth Cherry, PETITIONERS-APPELLANTS v. COMMISSIONER of Internal Revenue, RESPONDENT-APPELLEE. U.S. Court of Appeals, Second Circuit, Docket Nos. 83-4004—83-4006, Aug. 19, 1983. 79 TC 605 (No. 38) (opinion by Whitaker, *J.*) reversed. Years 1976-1977. Decision for Taxpayers.

1. NONDEDUCTIBLE ITEMS—Disallowance of certain expenses in connection with business use of home, rental of vacation homes, etc. Concert musicians at Metropolitan Opera allowed deduction for business use of residential areas. Although different from employer's principal place of business, focal point of employee's employment-related activities was practice areas in their home apartments. Private practice was essential to musicians but employer didn't provide practice space. *Reference:* 1983 P-H Fed. ¶16,982(5). Sec. 280A.

Stephen Gray, Michael L. Paup, Jonathan S. Cohen, Attys., Glenn L. Archer, Jr., Asst. Atty. Gen., Tax Div., Dept. of Justice, Wash., D.C., for Respondent-Appellee.

Before KAUFMAN, VAN GRAAFEILAND and PRATT, Circuit Judges.

Consolidated appeals from United States Tax Court judgments denying appellants home office deductions. I.R.C. §280A. Reversed and remanded.

VAN GRAAFEILAND, Circuit Judge:

An oft-repeated, perhaps apocryphal, story tells of the musician who, when asked the best way to get to Carnegie Hall, replied, "Practice! Practice!" Whether the story is truth or fiction, the fact remains that, for a performing musician, practice is not simply the best way to get to Carnegie Hall, it is the only way. It is the only way to get there, and it is the only way to ensure that, having arrived, one stays there. Ignace Paderewski, the famous pianist, once said:

> If I don't practice for one day, I know it; if I don't practice for two days, the critics know it; if I don't practice for three days, the audience knows it.

Elyse Mach, Great Pianists Speak For Themselves (Introduction by Sir Georg Solti XIV) (1980).

Since a musician must practice, he must have a place in which he can practice. This appeal concerns the tax treatment of portions of residential areas which are set aside and used solely for such purpose.

Ernest Drucker, Patricia Rogers, and Philip Cherry are concert musicians employed by the Metropolitan Opera Association, Inc. (the Met). During the period relevant to this appeal, each of them lived in a New York City apartment in which one room or a portion of a room was set aside and used exclusively for musical study and practice. Appellants spent approximately thirty to thirty-two hours per week studying and practicing in the areas reserved for such use, and this appears to be about average for musical artists. See, e.g., Mach, supra, at 9, 14, 63. On their tax returns,

Arthur Pelikow, Richard B. Sherman, N.Y., N.Y., Attys. for Petitioners-Appellants.

61,501

— P-H EXPLANATION ———

CROSS REFERENCE TABLES
CONTENTS

SUPPLEMENTARY CROSS REFERENCE TABLE

≫→ **Main Cross Reference Table begins at page 61,531.** ←≪

HOW TO USE THIS TABLE EFFECTIVELY

1. Start with the paragraph number of your subject.
2. Find the number in the table below in the column headed "From ¶"
3. Look opposite the number in the column headed "To ¶" There you will find the paragraph number of each related item concerning you.

Supplementary Cross Reference Table   **61,507**

From	To	
16,981 . . .	60,308	Treasury amends Prop. Regs on home office and home business use deductions. Ed
16,982(5). .	57,994	*Proskauer:* Business use of home owned by corp. TCMem
	58,043	*Alman:* Home office expense. TCMem
	58,097	*Harris:* Teacher's home office expense. TCMem
	58,154	*Batson:* Storage of supplies in dwelling. TCMem
	58,169	*Naggar:* Apartment used only for business on weekdays. TCMem
	60,350	Concert musicians allowed deductions for practice areas in their homes. Ed
	83-5223	*Drucker* rev: Employer didn't provide musicians with practice space. CA
16,982(10) .	57,974	*Buchholz:* Unit in condominium operated as hotel. TCMem
	58,010	*Bindseil:* Fair rental value of house rented to parents. TCMem
17,011 . . .	55,104	Adjustable or floating rate convertible notes. RevRul
17,031 . . .	60,280	IRS rules that adjustable rate convertible notes are equity. Ed
17,037(25) .	58,052	*E-B Grain Co., et al:* Final day of grace period on weekend. TC
17,037(90) .	. . . . . .	*Ocean Sands Holding Corp., et al v Comm.,* aff by unpublished order 2-11-83 CA 4; cert filed (T)
17,082(30) .	60,337	Corp. won deduction for loan guaranty fees paid to shareholder-directors. Ed
	83-5186	*Tulia Feedlot, Inc.:* Fee for personal guaranty of corp.'s debt by stockholder. ClCt
17,089(2). .	57,968	*Uranga:* Expenses incurred by corp. for benefit of shareholder. TCMem
17,089(10) .	. . . . . .	*Ocean Sands Holding Corp., et al v Comm.,* aff by unpublished order 2-11-83 CA 4; cert filed (T)
	57,951	*Parker Tree Farms, Inc., et al:* Use of auto was constructive dividend. TCMem
	58,026	*Smith, M.D., P.C.:* Shareholder use of corporate vehicle. TCMem
17,089(90) .	. . . . . .	*Ocean Sands Holding Corp., et al v Comm.,* aff by unpublished order 2-11-83 CA 4; cert filed (T)
17,093(5). .	57,951	*Parker Tree Farms, Inc., et al:* Repayment of loan was constructive dividend. TCMem
	57,968	*Uranga:* Constructive dividend in form of loan. TCMem
17,201 . . .	55,118	Dividend reinvestment plans for qualified public utilities. Intro TD
	60,290	Temporary and Prop. Regs cover dividend reinvestment in stock of public utilities. Ed
	60,361	Public hearing on dividend reinvestment in public utility stock set for 10-5-83. Ed

1983 P-H FEDERAL TAXES

Report Bulletin 39
Volume LXIV
In Three Sections: Section 1
September 8, 1983

Prentice-Hall, Inc. Englewood Cliffs, N.J. • 60,591

This Report includes the Tax Savings Series booklet "Tax Tips for Professionals" (Section 3).

Concert Musicians Allowed Deductions for Practice Areas in Their Homes

[¶ 60,350]   The Second Circuit Court of Appeals has just reversed the Tax Court and allowed concert musicians home-office deductions for the business use of their apartments. The court said that since the musicians' use of home studios for musical practice was a business necessity and was for the convenience of their employer which didn't provide practice space, the expenses for the area in their homes used for this purpose were deductible. Drucker, et al. v. Commissioner, 52 AFTR2d 83-5804.

Musicians spent most practice time at home. Ernest Drucker, Patricia Rogers and Philip Cherry were concert musicians employed by the New York Metropolitan Opera who spent less than half their working time at Lincoln Center. Each one spent about 30 hours per week studying and practicing their music in a part of their apartment set aside exclusively for such use and deducted the rent and costs allocable to the practice areas. Their work at rehearsals and performances was only possible after extensive solo practice with their instruments. The Met didn't provide the musicians with space for the essential task of private practice.

Musicians' principal places of business were their apartment practice studios. The Tax Court had determined that the musicians' principal place of business was the same as that of their employer, i.e., Lincoln Center. But the Second Circuit said that the Tax Court was wrong to rigidly apply such terms as "principal place of business" and "trade" to the musicians in light of unique

61,001

LIST OF CURRENT DECISIONS AND RULINGS

CONTENTS

All references are to PARAGRAPH [¶] NUMBERS   ● Supreme Court
For complete citations and judicial history, consult P-H Federal Tax Citator.
* Indicates paragraph [¶] numbers in P-H Memo TC

SUPPLEMENTARY LIST OF CURRENT DECISIONS
—— A — B — C ——

Adak Carting, Inc., *83,531 ..58,137
Adams, Frances Lee, Est. of v U.S. (See Swillinger, Melvin v U.S., 83-5173)

Barnhill, Margarita, *83,375 ..57,970
Barrow, John Guy, *83,123, app dis 7-13-83 CA 11 (T) ..57,692
Barry, Norman C. v U.S., DC, Ill. ..83-5099

Deak-Perera & Co.; U.S., et al v, DCDC ..83-5222
Deak-Perera & Co.; U.S., et al v, DCDC ..83-5128
Dean, Jack, Est. of, et al, *83,276 ..57,869
De Angeles, Ronald E., *83,078, pending CA 11 (T) ..57,641
Delaney, Ernest N., *82,666, pending CA 9 (T) ..57,155
Del Norte Natural Gas Co., *83,454 ..58,054
Denison, Cleo S. v Barlow, et al, DC, Ark. ..83-5093
Denison Poultry & Egg Co. v U.S., DC, Tex. ..83-5028
DeRosa, Vincent J. (See G&G Records, Inc., et al, 57,936)
● Desert Palace, Inc. v Comm., USCA 9, cert filed 5-6-83 (T) ..83-349
DeVenney, John J.; U.S., et al v (See Smith, J. D.; U.S., et al v, 83-5227)
Devon, Edward Buffington, *83,565 ..58,177
Dickman, Kenneth W., *83,484 ..58,085
DiFlorio, David G. v U.S., DC, N.Y. ..83-5194
Diggs, Charles C., Jr. v Comm., USCA 6 ..83-5236
DiPalmo, Rocco, *83,493 ..58,096
Ditunno, Anthony J., 80 TC 362, pending CA 6 (G) ..57,622
Doan, Joseph L., Jr.; U.S. v, USCA 3 ..83-5165
Dobrochowski, Charles F., *83,269 ..57,855
Dodge, Charles A., *83,431 ..58,031
Dolan, T. Frank, Jr. v U.S., DC, N.Y. ..83-5195
● Dowell, Alfonzo L. v Comm., 45 AFTR2d 80-855, cert filed 5-19-83 (G)
Drefke, Paul M.; U.S. v, USCA 8 ..83-5010
Dreher, Michael P., *83,499 ..58,102
● Drey, Leo A. v U.S., USCA 8, cert filed 6-20-83 (T) ..83-437
Driscoll, Daniel G. v U.S. (See DiFlorio, David G. v U.S., 83-5194)
Drucker, Ernest v Comm., USCA 2 ..83-5223

E-B Grain Co., et al, 81 TC No. 6 ..58,052
Eblen, George C., et al, *82,448, pending CA 6 (T)
Ecclesiastical Order of the Ism of Am. Inc; The, 00 TO 033, pending CA 6 (T) ..57,827
Edler, Vernon, Jr., *82,067, app auth CA 9
Farrah, William J.; U.S. v, USCA 6 ..83-5240
Farrell, Paul, *83,542 ..58,149
Felkel, S. E. v U.S., DC, S.C. ..83-5056
Fellner, Andrew T.; Hammond Co., The, et al v (See Hammond Co., The v U.S., 83-5181)
Fenton, Jerold Norman, *83,410 ..58,009
Fields, Jack D. v Comm., aff by unpublished order 8-29-83 CA 9; *81,653
● Fifth Third Bk., The (Rush, Kenneth G. v U.S.), v U.S., USCA 6, cert den 6-13-83 (T); rehg den 1-21-83 ..83-328
Finer, Albert J.; U.S., et al v, USCA 10 ..83-5049
Finley, James, *83,295 ..57,890
First Chicago Corp., 80 TC 648, app auth CA7 ..57,762
First Nat. Bank of Chicago, The; U.S., et al v, USCA 7, no cert ..83-432
First Nat. Bk. of Valdosta v Elgin, J. Tom, DC Fla. ..83-5153
First Nat. Bk. of Valdosta v U.S. (See First Nat. Bk. of Valdosta v Elgin, J. Tom, 83-5153)
First Nat. Bk.; U.S., et al v, DC, Iowa ..83-5061
First Western Govt. Securities, Inc.; U.S., et al v (See Samuels, Kramer & Co., et al; U.S., et al v, 83-5208)
Fisher, Johnny Joe, In re, BktCt, Kan. ..83-5095
Fitzsimmons, James A.; U.S. v, USCA 7 ..83-5189
Flomenhoft, Howard C.; U.S. v, USCA 7 ..83-5190
Fla. Trade Exchange, Inc.; U.S., et al v (See Gottlieb, Herbert; U.S., et al v, 83-5237)
Flowers, George T., et al, 80 TC 914 ..57,858
Foglesong, Frederick H. v Comm., 50 AFTR2d 82-6016. no cert ..56,578

PART III

How to Find the Solution To a Tax Problem

To solve any federal tax problem, begin with Prentice-Hall's Federal Taxes, that part of the Prentice-Hall Federal Tax Equipment illustrated on page 26. This is the place to begin whether your problem arises from a mere statement of facts, or question of law, or if you have to prepare a return, refund claim, deficiency letter, petition to a court, or a brief. The best way to illustrate the use of the Federal Taxes Service is by working out an actual tax problem.

The P-H Federal Taxes Service offers a choice of methods for finding information. The solution can be approached by Code section number or by subject. If you know the Code section number, you can go directly to the text. If you don't know the Code section number, you can proceed by subject matter either directly to the text by means of key words, or through the Index. All three methods will be explained. But first let's set up the problem to be researched.

PROBLEM 1

The problem involves a musician for an opera company, who must spend time practicing his music to do his job properly. His employer provides no space for the practice. The musician spends most of his working time practicing in his apartment, where he has set aside one room for this exclusive use. He spends most of the rest of his working time at rehearsals or performances at the opera house. Some time is also spent in performance at other locations and on tour and, during the musician's summer vacation, for other employers.

Question: Can the musician deduct the rent, electricity and maintenance costs that are allocable to the area of his apartment used for practice?

The answer depends mainly on whether Sec. 280A would apply to disallow the deduction. Let's see if careful research in the Federal Taxes Service can provide an answer. Our research will use the three methods previously mentioned: Code section, Key Word and Index.

CODE SECTION METHOD

In order to use the Code section method to solve the illustrative problem you need to know that Sec. 280A deals with restrictions on home-office deductions.

The Service is arranged in Code Section order. The backbones of the Service volumes show that Sec. 280A is covered in Volume 4. The Tab (divider) cards of Volume 4 *(pictured on page 38)* show that Code Sec. 280A is covered in the 16,500 Tab. In the Finding List of Code and Regulation Sections which follows the tab card and the Topical Table of Contents *(see page 39)*, you will find that Code Sec. 280A is at ¶16,981.15. Turn to the P-H Explanation ¶16,981 *(page 41)*, which immediately precedes Sec. 280A.

P-H Explanation ¶16,981 deals with the topic "Disallowance of Certain Expenses in Connection With Business Use of Home, Rental of Vacation Homes, Etc." The bold face (heavy print) subheading entitled "(a) Home office deduction" tells you that self-employed persons and employees can't take any home office deductions unless the costs deducted are allocable to a part of the home used exclusively and on a regular basis as the principal place of business for any trade or business of the taxpayer's, or unless one of two other tests is met. It also notes that an employee must further prove that the exclusive use of the home-office is for the convenience of the employer. It cites Code Sec. 280A(c)(1) and refers you to ¶16,982(5) for details.

At ¶16,982(5) *(page 43)* you find numerous cases dealing with taxpayers who tried to deduct expenses of a home office where they prepared for their occupation. In most of these cases the IRS prevailed. For example in *Randolph Baie*, the Tax Court denied a home office deduction to a hot dog stand proprietor for business use of a kitchen and bookkeeping room in her residence because the hot dog stand was the principal place of business. This is a good time to point out that your research is not complete until you have checked the Current Matter Volume of your Service (Volume 11) for the latest developments, if any, on your question.

To check if there are any current developments, turn to the Cross Reference Tables to New Developments (Tab 61,500, Vol. 11). In the Main Cross Reference Table that starts on page 61,531 *(page 44)* you check for ¶16,982(5) in the left hand "From ¶" column and scan the area entitled "Disallowance of Certain Expenses in Connection with Business Use of Home, Rental of Vacation Homes, Etc." for any related developments that may affect the home office deduction claim. You find three Tax Court memorandum cases dealing with home practice rooms of concert musicians. The cases are *Drucker, Rogers* and *Cherry*. When you turn to the digests of these decisions at ¶57,034; 57,054 and 57,055 you discover that in all of them the Tax Court denied the home office deduction and that the Court in the *Cherry* and *Rogers* cases cited *Drucker*. The *Drucker* case held that the musician's principal place of business was the opera house where he rehearsed and performed. If you turn to the texts of the *Cherry* and *Rogers* cases in P-H Tax Court Reported and Memorandum Decisions at ¶82,578 and 82,579 you discover that both these cases also cited the *Baie* case for the principal that the "focal point" of the taxpayer's activities determined his principal place of business.

For a final check of the very latest developments go to the Supplementary Cross Reference Table that starts on page 61,501. Opposite ¶16,982(5) in the "From ¶" column of the table *(shown on page 46)*, you will find that the *Drucker* case was reversed by a decision at ¶83-5223 of the AFTR2d Decisions Volume of Federal Taxes. You will also find an article at ¶60,350 dealing with the reversal. When you turn to the text of the decision you learn from the P-H headnote that the Second Circuit held that home practice was the "focal point" of the musician's activities, and was for the convenience of the employer. You also learn that the Second Circuit's opinion also reversed appeals from the *Rogers* and *Cherry* cases, which had been consolidated with *Drucker*. Advance sheets that included the full text of the Second Circuit *Drucker* case were included in the 83-5000 tab of the AFTR2d Decisions Volume. The case will appear in AFTR2d Series bound volume No. 52 when that volume is published. The case will be cited as 52 AFTR2d 83-5804.

The Service Report Bulletins contain summary digests of cases, and developments that relate to them, in the part of the Bulletin entitled "This Week's Tax News." A brief digest of the Second Circuit *Drucker* decision appeared in Report Bulletin 39, dated 9-8-83. You can also check for current developments as to cases and rulings by case name or ruling number, in the List of Current Decisions and Rulings *(page 48)*.

KEY WORD METHOD

In this method you choose a key word that is related to the problem from the backbones of the volumes. In this case your most likely key word is "Home office". Since there's no entry for it on the backbones (it's impossible for practical reasons to include all main topics there), check your key words in the index (Volume 1), and proceed as discussed in the "Index Method", below.

INDEX METHOD

The question suggests the following words as possible entry points into the index (tab 100 of Volume 1 of the Service).

Home office

Home

The bold face (heavy-print) index heading "Home office expenses" directs you to "Residential property, business use in part." Under the bold face index heading "Residential property" and the subtopic "business use in part" the index line "expense" directs you to ¶16,981(a); 16,981.15 and 16,982(5). References to paragraph numbers in the index are in bold face if they are references to a Code Section and in italics if they refer to a Regulation. Thus you can tell at a glance that ¶16,981.15 is the location of a Code Section.

The index line "business use in part" under the bold face index heading "Home" directs you to ¶16,981(a); 16,981.15 and 16,982(3) and (5).

The index line "office in personal residence" under the bold face (heavy-print) index heading "Business expenses" directs you to ¶16,981(a); 16,981.15 and 16,982(5).

The reference to ¶16,981(a) pinpoints the location of your search. By turning to that subparagraph you can proceed with your research in the same way as under the Code Section method. Index references to ¶16,981.15 locate Code Sec. 280A and references to ¶16,982(5) locate the case law relating to the restrictions on home office deductions. Use the research techniques explained under the Code Section method to check for current developments.

PROBLEM 2

In the second problem we show how flexible indexing in P-H FEDERAL TAXES permits you to use one or more of the secondary finding aids such as Pilot Charts and Transaction Index Tables.

Question. Can a professional group—doctors, lawyers or accountants, organize its business in such a way as to be recognized as a corporation for tax purposes?

The professional corporation question presents a special kind of research problem because it involves a consideration of taxable entities: what characteristics must a group or association possess so that it will be recognized as a corporation for tax purposes. P-H Federal Taxes has a special section in Volume 8 devoted to the discussion of general principles such as the classification of taxpayers and the effect of state laws.

The discussion of professional corporations is in the "General Principles—Taxpayers Classified—Definitions—Code Sec 7701 tab of Volume 8, at ¶41,628 in the compilation. The words "General Principles" are on the backbone of Volume 8. And there are numerous references in the index leading to that paragraph. For example, under each of the headings "attorneys", "doctors" and "professional people" there is a line "corporate status benefits . . . ¶41,628." But, let's assume that we could not find a specific reference to the paragraph.

Pilot Charts. These charts begin each principal division of Federal Taxes dealing with income tax. They furnish in condensed form a complete summary of the entire contents covered under a particular tab card. If you know the information you seek is under a subject covered by a particular tab, reference to the chart will frequently locate the information, if the index can't.

Turn to the Pilot Chart for the General Principles tab *(see below and page 53)*. Looking down the chart you find under "Taxpayers Classified" a statement about professional corporations and a reference to ¶41,628.

Pilot Chart   41,003

[¶41,000] ●**Pilot Chart—General Principles—Taxpayers Classified—Definitions.**

SUBSTANCE V. FORM	**The rule** is that the substance of a transaction rather than the form controls tax liability. ¶41,001. **The Supreme Court** has stated and applied the rule in various ways. ¶41,002. **A tax avoidance** motive may give rise to the application of this rule but the motive alone does establish liability. ¶41,005. **Other transactions** which may give rise to this application include: (1) Transactions not at arm's length. ¶41,007. (2) Sales which establish losses. ¶41,008. (3) Transactions between controlling stockholders and corporation. ¶41,010. (4) Corporate reorganizations. ¶41,011. (5) Transactions involving several steps. ¶41,012. (6) Rents as distinguished from sales. ¶41,018.

EFFECT OF STATE LAWS	**Generally** the Code and the Federal Courts define and interpret the tax law. ¶41,101. **The Supreme Court** has laid down the general principles of the effect of State laws on the tax law. In essence there is a desire to give uniform application to Federal law unless there is express language or implication to the contrary. ¶41,102. **The instances** where State law may be used in determining certain tax consequences include: (1) Where there are undefined words and there is an implication that the interpretation is to be found in State law. ¶41,105. (2) Certain features in taxing estates, trusts, and beneficiaries. ¶41,109. (3) Certain rights and interests. ¶41,107. **Exemption laws and statutes of limitations** are generally not applicable. ¶41,111.

The intention of the legislature in passing a tax statute may be found in committee reports; court decisions; regulations and rulings. ¶41,351.

Until the Supreme Court has finally decided a matter, the IRS is not required to follow any court decision. They may follow their own rulings. ¶41,359; 41,360; 41,361.

INTERPRE- TATION OF TAX STATUTES	**Regulations and T.D.s** (Treasury Decisions) have the force and effect of laws. However, if they are not correct interpretations of the law, the courts need not follow them. Other rulings do not have this effect. ¶41,355; 41,357; 41,363; 41,365; 41,368; 41,457.

TAXPAYERS CLASSIFED

CLASSIFICA- TION IN GENERAL	**The Code separates taxpayers** into various groups for tax purposes. Common examples are individuals, corporations, estates and trusts. Since the taxing provisions of the Code are not uniform for all classes, the first thing to do is find out how you are classifed. The kind of return you file, the rates that apply and your rights and duties as a taxpayer depend on it. ¶41,601. **The standards you use** in classifying an organization are supplied by Federal, not local, law. Local or common labels are not controlling. However, you may look to local law to determine if the characteristics of your organization are such that the standards are met. ¶41,608. Some states now permit professional groups to incorporate under the so-called professional corporation or association laws. See ¶41,628.
ASSOCIA- TIONS	**"Associations"** are taxed the same as corporations. ¶41,615. Generally speaking, an association is an organization that resembles a corporation more than it resembles some other form of organization. ¶41,615. More specifically, an association is an organization that has associates, a business purpose, and such corporate characteristics as centralized management, continuity of existence, transferable interests and limited liability. ¶41,616; 41,617 et seq.

Transaction Index. This consists of various tax situations arranged according to the way they affect common, everyday business transactions. Along with a check list of the things you should know about a transaction, there are references to paragraphs in the compilation where you will find complete discussions of the listed topics. This unique index is in Volume 1 of P-H Federal Taxes. Start with the Table of Contents on pages 1002 and 1003. Going through the list of transaction tables you find an article on "Professional Practitioners" at ¶1125.

TABLE OF CONTENTS

Turning to ¶1125 we find that there is a check list of the tax factors that every professional person must consider. One of the items mentioned is "Professional corporations" with a brief description of the topic and a reference to the complete discussion at ¶41,608.

PROFESSIONAL PRACTITIONERS

[¶1125]   This explanation deals with individuals who are practicing a profession. Practice usually involves maintaining an office individually or as a member of a partnership, and receiving fees for particular services rendered to clients or patients. The group includes, among others, lawyers, accountants, doctors, dentists, architects, and engineers.

Professional corporations.—Organizations of doctors, lawyers, and other professional individuals organized under state professional association acts will generally be treated as corporations for tax purposes. You may want to consider such employee fringe benefits as medical reimbursement plans, group insurance, disability payments, etc., if you choose to operate as a professional corporation . . . . ¶41,628 ←

Conclusion. At ¶41,628 we learn that IRS concedes that organizations of professional people organized under state professional association acts will generally be treated as corporations for tax purposes, but that the relative tax advantage of incorporation by professionals has been reduced by law changes designed to equalize the benefits of Keogh plans and corporate plans. See page 55.

PROFESSIONAL SERVICE ASSOCIATIONS

P-H EXPLANATION

¶41,628 **Basic rules.**—In response to recent decisions, (5) below, IRS now concedes that organizations of doctors, lawyers, and other professional people organized under state professional association acts will generally be treated as corporations for tax purposes. This action followed a decision not to apply to the Supreme Court for certiorari on *O'Neill* and *Kurzner*, (5) below, where the 6th and 5th Circuits held that a group of doctors organized under state law was classifiable as a corporation for Federal tax purposes. An earlier decision was made not to seek certiorari in *Empey*, (5) below, where the 10th Circuit held that a group of lawyers organized under the general corporation laws of Colorado to be a corporation for Federal tax purposes. And IRS has conformed to the above decisions by revoking certain provisions in Reg. §301.7701-1 and §301.7701-2 relating to the tax classification of professional service organizations. IRS has considered the laws of each state and ruled that groups legally organized under professional association acts in every state (except D.C.) will qualify as corporations for tax purposes. Thus in most cases qualification as a corporation is now automatic. Furthermore, groups organized under the general business corporations laws of each state will generally qualify. For the list of state statutes ruled on by IRS, see *RevRul 70-101*, as amplified and modified, (5) below.

The main tax advantage that spurred the use of the professional corporation, was the relatively more liberal treatment accorded to corporate qualified retirement plans then to retirement plans that cover self-employed persons (Keogh plans). Corporate retirement plans had been more liberally treated as to limitations on and deductibility of contributions, and as to taxation of benefits and distributions. ¶19,700; 19,720. Self-employed individuals also wanted to be treated as "actual employees," in order to reap employee benefits which include also (1) tax-free sick pay [¶8364]; (2) tax deductible life insurance premiums [¶16,765; 16,766]; and (3) tax-free $5,000 death benefit [¶8151].

The relative tax advantage of incorporation by professionals has, however, been reduced in 1982 by law changes designed to equalize the tax benefits of Keogh plans and corporate plans. See ¶19,005; 19,577. Also under Sec. 269A the IRS can now reallocate income, deductions and cred-

---

STATES ALLOWING ALL PROFESSIONALS TO INCORPORATE.—Alabama; Alaska; Arizona; Arkansas; Delaware; District of Columbia; Florida; Idaho; Illinois; Indiana; Kentucky; Maine; Maryland; Michigan; Mississippi; Nebraska; Nevada; New Jersey; New Mexico; New York; North Dakota; Oregon; Pennsylvania; South Carolina; Tennessee; Texas; Vermont; Virginia; Washington; Wisconsin; Wyoming.

STATES LIMITING PROFESSIONAL CORPORATIONS TO CERTAIN PROFESSIONALS.—California; Colorado; Connecticut; Georgia; Hawaii; Iowa; Kansas; Louisiana; Massachusetts; Minnesota; Missouri; Montana; New Hampshire; North Carolina; Ohio; Oklahoma; Rhode Island; South Dakota; Utah; West Virginia.

PART IV

Additional Research Aids

In the preceding parts of the booklet we described the elements of a complete tax library and illustrated the use of the equipment by taking you through the solution of two actual tax problems. In this last part we have set down a number of additional research aids—alternate ways to approach problems that can save you time and add depth and quality to your research.

TRANSACTION INDEX

Tax research can—and frequently does—*start* with a Transaction Index Table (see page 57). It is a type of index, organizing all of the tax aspects of many common situations or transactions. These transactions are arranged alphabetically, and under each one is an analysis of the tax problems affecting it, with references leading to paragraphs in Federal Taxes where these aspects are fully discussed. Each Transaction analysis includes or leads to practical and tested tax saving suggestions.

Suppose, you are drawing up a real estate lease. You want to make sure that you will take into account all possible tax contingencies that might arise. Your problem is too general to locate through the alphabetical index *quickly* (because *you* have to think of each tax contingency).

The Transaction Index in Volume 1 is your answer. It notes every possible tax contingency that could arise in your situation, and leads you to specific paragraphs in **FEDERAL TAXES** that tell you what to do about them.

Partial List of Transaction Indexes

Accidents	Corporations:	Leasing machinery and
Advance payments	General discussion	equipment
Amortization	Affiliated	Minerals
Appreciation in value of	Closely held	Mortgages
property	Liquidations	Officers of corporations
Authors, composers, and	Partnerships compared	Partnerships—limited
other artists	Formation	partnerships
Automobiles	Damages	Patents and copyrights
Bankruptcy	Dealers	Professional practitioners
Bargain purchases and	Employment contracts	Purchase of property
sales	Estates of decedents	Real estate:
Beneficiaries	Family transactions	Acquisition ownership
Bonuses	Farmers	disposition
Books and records	Fiduciaries	Leases
Buying or selling a going	Films and tapes	Residential
corporation	Foreign exchange	Relatives
Buying or selling a	Franchises	Retailers
proprietorship	Fringe benefits	Sales and exchanges of
Buying or selling	Furniture and fixtures	property
partnership interests	Goodwill and covenants	Senior citizens
Carrying or financing	not to compete	Stocks and securities:
charges	Guaranty	Bonds
Checks	Guardians	Stocks
Children	Husband and wife	Trade-ins
Collection	Inventions	Trusts—creation
Commissions	Investors	Veterans
Constructive income and	Joint ownership of	
payments	property	

Prentice-Hall Transaction Index

REAL ESTATE—ACQUISITION, OWNERSHIP AND DISPOSITION

[¶1129] Many sections of the income tax law affect real estate. Almost everything you do from the time you buy it until you sell it affects the amount of your income tax bill. Some things that just happen affect it too, e.g., real estate is damaged, destroyed or condemned. Each time you do something or something happens, check the lists below to find the effect on your income tax bill. See also ¶1127 above and 1133 below.

Events that affect real estate owners are listed below under the following headings: income or loss at time of acquisition; receipts during ownership; disbursements during ownership; sale or other disposition and basis for gain or loss or depreciation.

Special rules for low-income housing are explained at ¶31,799.

As to *new liberal writeoffs for real estate* under ACRS depreciation, see ¶15,004.

(a) Income or loss at time of acquisition.—An ordinary purchase or any one of the following transactions generally involves no recognized gain or loss:

Acquired by bequest, devise or inheritance .... ¶8181
Acquired in exchange for other business real estate of like kind ... ¶31,655
Contributed by consumers to induce erection of facility .... ¶8666

Income may be realized or loss sustained if the property is acquired by one of the following methods:

Accepted in debt settlement .... ¶14,770; 31,108
Compensation for services .... ¶7071
Liquidating dividend from corporation .... ¶17,576 et seq.
Mortgagee's acquisition by:
   Foreclosure sale .... ¶7227; 14,921; 20,445
   Voluntary surrender by mortgagor .... ¶7227; 14,921; 20,444; 31,108
   Repossession of property previously sold on installment or deferred payment
   plan .... ¶20,443; 20,486

(d) Sale or other disposition.—Gain or loss is recognized on a sale or exchange of real estate unless expected by statute [¶31,010]. The amount of the gain or loss is the difference between the adjusted basis of the property (generally cost plus improvements less depreciation) and the amount realized [¶31,006]. Whether the gain or loss upon a sale or exchange is treated as a capital gain or loss or as an ordinary gain or loss usually depends upon the purpose for which the property is held [¶32,471]. For possible recapture of depreciation, see ¶32,761.

However, if a person 65 or over at time of sale sells his residence at a gain, all or part of his gain is tax-free .... ¶8705
Abandonment .... ¶14,243
Casualty—fire, flood, storm, etc. .... ¶14,361 et seq.; 32,231; 32,248
Condemnation .... ¶31,712; 32,248
Crops, unharvested .... ¶32,275
Cutting of timber .... ¶22,431
Deferred payment sale:
   Installment plan (no initial payment or initial payments not in excess of
   30% of sales price) .... ¶20,415 et seq.

OTHER APPROACHES TO FEDERAL TAX PROBLEMS

In addition to the Code section, key words, or the index method of approach, the tax practitioner may approach the problem from many other angles. Or he or she may have the name of a case or number of a ruling and want to go directly to the place where all the material relating to it will appear.

Prentice-Hall's **FEDERAL TAXES** includes many special features to help you approach a problem from these and other angles. These features are shown on the chart below and opposite, and are fully illustrated on the following pages, as indicated on the chart.

IF YOU WANT—	USE THIS SPECIAL FEATURE
More information about a Tax Court or other court decision of which you know the name.	The List of Decisions in Volume 1, tab 1500 and Volume 11, tab 61,000. List is illustrated at pages 59 & 60.
More information about a tax ruling of which you know the identifying number; e.g., Rev. Proc. 64-21.	The Rulings finding Lists in Volume 1, tab 1300 and Volume 11, tab 61,000. Illustrated on page 61.
Analysis of law; a quick summary of the law on a certain subject, e.g., Capital Gains & Losses, Dividends, Deduction of Losses.	Pilot Charts. There is one following the Table of Contents for nearly every tab card. Illustrated on page 62.
To determine the weight the courts will give to the authorities you are relying on.	Interpretation of Tax Statutes, Volume 10, tab 41,000. Illustrated on page 63.
Complete information on a general principle of law, such as "Substance v. Form," " Effect of State law," etc.	The General Principles division, Volume 10, tab 41,000. Material is explained and illustrated on page 64.
To know what items are taxable, nontaxable, deductible, or nondeductible.	The Check Lists, Volume 1, tab 1200. Illustrated on page 65.
An index to the major subdivisions of any tax problem.	"Boxes" in the Index, Volume 1, tab 100. Illustrated on page 66.
Information on an election.	Tax Elections Checklist, Volume 1, tab 1,000. Illustrated on page 67.
Rates of tax.	The Tax Rate Tables, Volume 1, tab 3100. Illustrated on page 68.
To know what tax experts have written about the tax problem *you* have.	The Index to Tax Articles, Volume 1, tab 2900. Material explained and illustrated on page 69.
The *full text* of any provision of the Internal Revenue Code or tax regulations as they apply to a prior taxable year.	The Cumulative Changes Service, fully explained on pages 31 thru 33.

TABLE OF CASES

The Table of Cases lists alphabetically all the decisions cited in the text of the Federal Taxes Service, and the numbers of the paragraphs at which they appear. A table of current cases, issued after the text was printed, appears in Volume 11.

An extract from the Table of Cases is shown below. The arrows point out some of the features of the table.

1. U.S. Supreme Court Decisions are indicated by a black "bullet." (See Amer. Hide & Leather Co. v. U.S.).

2. Citation to Amer. Light & Traction Co. (3 TC 1048) cites a TC bound volume. There is also a note (A) which indicates that the Commissioner has acquiesced in this case. Amer. Liberty Oil Co. (43 BTA 76) includes the symbols "A, NA" which indicates that the Commissioner has acquiesced on some points and not on others. Citation to the appropriate cumulative bulletin is also included.

3. Memorandum Decisions from the Board of Tax Appeals and Tax Court are listed (see Amer.-La France Foamite Corp., ¶59,101 P-H Memo TC).

1518—Fed. Cases　　　　**AMER.—AMER.**　　　　[9]
——————— For complete citations and judicial history consult P-H Federal Tax Citator ———————

Amer. Gas & Elec. Secur. Corp. v Comm (See Nat. Secur. Corp. v Comm.)

Amer. Gas Machine Co. v U.S. (See Junior Toy Corp. v U.S.)

Amer. Gen. Ins. Co. v U.S., 32 AFTR2d 73-5808 ..7206(80); 29,139; 29,196; 36,026(5)

Amer. Gilsonite Co., 28 TC 194 (NA, 1964-1 CB 6) ..22,235(70); 22,259(15); 22,272(45)

Amer. Gilsonite Co.; Comm. v, 259 F2d 654, 2 AFTR2d 5876 ..22,235(70); 22,259(15); 22,272(45)

Amer. Glass Co., *39,485 ..14,890(15)

Amer. Glue Co. v U.S., 42 F2d 234, 8 AFTR 1106 (1930) ..36,028(5)

Amer. Gypsum Co., *44,094 ..17,368(5)

Amer. Hardware & Equipment Co., *52,197 ..12,098(20)

Amer. Hardware & Equip. Co. v Comm., 202 F2d 126, 43 AFTR 277 (1953) ..12,098(20)

Amer. Health Studios, Inc., In re, 178 F Supp 553, 5 AFTR2d 602 ..37,695(25)

● Amer. Hide & Leather Co. v U.S., 284 US 598, 76 L Ed. 514, 52 S Ct 207 ..36,123(5); 36,575(30); 36,576(15)

● Amer. Hide & Leather Co. v U.S., 284 US 343, 76 L Ed. 331, 52 S Ct 154, 10 AFTR 775, CB June 1932, p. 201 (1932) ..36,123(5); 36,575(30); 36,576(15)

Amer. Hide & Leather Co. v U.S., 75 Ct Cl 393, 58 F2d 1080, 11 AFTR 356 (1932) ..36,123(5); 36,575(30); 36,576(15)

Amer. Hide & Leather Co. v U.S., 71 Ct Cl 114, 48 F2d 430, 9 AFTR 1118 (1930) ..36,123(5); 36,575(30); 36,576(15)

Amer.-La France-Foamite Corp., *59,101 ..14,734(40)

Amer.-La France-Foamite Corp. v Comm., 284 F2d 723, 6 AFTR2d 6056 ..14,734(40)

Amer. Land & Invest. Co., 14 BTA 615 ..20,241(5); 20,426(45)

Amer. Land & Invest. Co., Ex. (Hester) v Comm., 40 F2d 336, 8 AFTR 10738 (1930) ..20,241(5); 20,426(45)

Amer. Laundry Machinery Co., 32 BTA 793 ..13,155

Amer. Lawn Mower Co. v U.S., 12 AFTR2d 6162 ..20,910(35); 21,334

Amer. Liberty Oil Co., 1 TC 386 ..36,465(70)

Amer. Liberty Oil Co., 43 BTA 76 (A, NA, CB 1944, p. 2, 32) ..7534(10); 13,287(15); 17,597(150); 20,607(10); 31,219(5)

Amer. Liberty Oil Co.; Comm. v, 127 F2d 262, 29 AFTR 245 (1942) ..7534(10); 13,287(15); 17,597(150); 20,-607(10); 31,219(5)

Amer. Liberty Oil Co. v Comm., CCA 5, ¶ 61,027 P-H 1944 Fed ..36,465(70)

Amer. Liberty Pipe Line Co., 2 TC 309 ..20,684(5); 41,028

Amer. Liberty Pipe Line Co. v Comm., 143 F2d 873, 32 AFTR 1099 (1944) ..20,684(5); 41,028

Amer. Light & Traction Co., 3 TC 1048 (A, CB 1946-2, p. 1) ..13,181; 13,295(25); 17,067(5)

Amer. Light & Traction Co., 42 BTA 1121 (NA, CB 1944, p. 32) ..33,940(5)

Amer. Light & Traction Co.; Comm. v, 156 F2d 398, 34 AFTR 1544(1946) ..13,181; 13,295(25); 17,067(5)

Amer. Light & Traction Co.; Comm. v, 125 F2d 365, 28 AFTR 1037 (1942) ..33,940(5)

● **Supreme Court Decisions**　　*Indicates Paragraph [¶] Number in P-H Memo TC Service

COURT PROCEEDINGS

The latest developments on cases reported currently and in the compilation can be checked in either of two ways: by case name in the Current Table of Cases, or by paragraph number in the Cross Reference Table to New Developments. Both of these tables are in Volume 11, the current matter volume.

Among the items shown are:

Whether Supreme Court review has been asked (cert filed)

Whether the Supreme Court has agreed to review (cert granted)

Whether an appeal is pending (pending CA)

Who is appealing: The government (G) or taxpayer (T)

Whether and when the appeal is dismissed (app dis)

The method of checking court proceedings by case name is illustrated in the extract below from the Current Table of Cases.

● **American Internat. Coal Co., Inc. v Comm.**, aff by unpublished order 3-8-83 CA 3; cert filed 6-27-83 (T); *82,204

Ameron, Inc. v U.S., aff in part, rev in part, rem in part by unpublished order 6-6-83 CA 9; 49 AFTR2d 82-323

Anderson, P.J. & Sons, *83,323 ..57,917

Anselmo, Ronald P., 80 TC 872, pending CA 11 (T) ..57,848

Anthes, David E., 81 TC No. 1 ..57,982

● **Ariz. Governing Committee for Tax Deferred Annuity & Deferred Compensation Plans, etc., et al v Norris, Nathalie etc.**, SCt ..83-5070

Berney, Peter E.; U.S., et al v, USCA 10 ..83-5179

Bershesky, Peter, *83,452 ..58,051

Bethel Conservative Mennonite Church, 80 TC 352, pending CA 7 (T) ..57,614

Bevitori, Clente A., *83,530 ..58,136

Bindseil, Lee A., *83,411 ..58,010

Birch, Rex D. v IRS, et al, DC, Wyo. ..83-5238

Bizub, Michael et al, *83,280 ..57,876

Black, Deborah Kay (See Dean, Jack, Est. of, et al, 57,869)

Blackmon, Dee O., *83,412 ..58,011

Blaser, Bonnie J., *81,070, app dis 7-7-83 CA 7 (T)

● **Bob Jones University v U.S.**, SCt ..83-5001

The check of court proceedings by paragraph number is made through the Cross Reference Table to New Developments. If the case you are checking is in the text of the Service, check the paragraph number in the text at which the case appears. Here is an extract from the Cross Reference Table.

16,982(5). .	. . . .	*Cousino, Paul W. v Comm.*, cert den 11-29-82 CA 6 (T)
	. . . . . .	*Moskovit, Leonard A.*, pending CA 10 (T)
	. . . . . .	*Warganz, Joseph F. v Comm.*, aff by unpublished order 10-15-82 CA 3
56,530		*Loughlin:* Mobilehome was dwelling unit; home office of pilot. DC
57,006		*Odom, Jr.:* Bedroom wasn't used exclusively for business. TCMem, aff by unpublished order 4-15-83 CA 4
57,019		*Smith:* No part of home used exclusively for office. TCMem
57,034		*Drucker:* Concert violinist's home practice room. TC, pending CA 2 (T)
57,052		*Anderson:* Anesthetist-farm owner's home office. TCMem
57,054		*Rogers:* Concert bassoonist's home practice room. TCMem, app dis 1-21-83 CA 2 (T)

If the case you are checking is in current matter, check the current paragraph number at which the case is reported. Example:

56,606	*CRC Corp. v Comm.*, cert den 6-6-83 CA 3 (T)
57,006	*Odom, Fitzhugh L., Jr. v Comm.*, aff by unpublished order 4-15-83 CA 4
57,022	*Friedland, Harold*, app dis 5-12-83 CA 3 (G)
57,034	*Drucker, Ernest*, pending CA 2 (T)
57,038	*Neil, Garnett W.*, pending CA 9 (T)
57,043	*Powers, George*, pending CA 7 (T)

TABLE OF RULINGS

The Table of Rulings is a finding list of Revenue Rulings, Revenue Procedures, Information Releases, Executive Orders, Treasury Decisions, Delegation Orders and other IRS rulings listed in the Table of Contents below.

How to use the main table.— When your research begins with the number of an IRS ruling whether referred to in another ruling or decision, periodical, conference or other source, references to compilation paragraphs in these tables take you to the digest of the ruling classified in accordance with related material with a reference to its published full text.

Current Table of Rulings.—This Main Table of Rulings is supplemented by the current table under the 61,000 tab in Volume 11. The current table lists all rulings added to "Federal Taxes" during the current year by publication in the Current Matter Volume.

⟦¶1300⟧

TABLE OF CONTENTS

PILOT CHARTS

Pilot Charts are a graphic resume of an area of federal tax law. By charting cumbersome legal provisions they present a quick comprehensive picture of an entire part (frequently a subchapter) of the Internal Revenue Code. They save the researcher's time whenever he or she knows the tab card division of P-H Federal Taxes covering the subject.

For example, suppose your client bought or sold real property. You know that deduction for real estate taxes paid must be apportioned. But how? Turn to the 13,000 tab in Volume 3. Flip a page. You quickly spot your item *(see arrow)* and find the detailed explanation at ¶13,283.

[¶13,000] ● **Pilot Chart—Deduction for Interest and Taxes.—**

INTEREST

DEFINITION	**Interest** is the amount which one has contracted to pay for the use of borrowed money. ¶13,003.
	Time for Deduction.—*Cash basis* taxpayers can deduct interest only in the year actually paid. ¶13,052. *Accrual basis* taxpayers must take deduction in the periods within which the liability to pay interest accrues, regardless of when payment is actually made. ¶13,067.

TAXES

DEFINITION	**A tax** is a charge made primarily for the purpose of raising revenue. It should be distinguished from a *fee* which covers charges for particular acts or services, from a *penalty* for nonpayment of taxes, and from a *capital expenditure.* ¶13,107 et seq.
	Taxes deductible as such.—This covers all State and local taxes, except estate, inheritance, legacy, succession, and gift taxes which are not deductible at all, and assessments for local benefits which are subject to special rules. It also covers the windfall profit tax, ¶191,601, *Excise Taxes.* State and local taxes on the sale of gasoline, diesel fuel, and other motor fuels are not deductible. ¶13,100; 13,265.
WHEN DEDUCTIBLE	**Generally,** a tax is deductible in the year "paid or accrued" depending upon whether the taxpayer is on the cash or accrual basis. ¶13,117. However, a taxpayer can elect to accrue real property taxes over the period, ¶20,599, and a special rule applies to both cash and accrual basis taxpayers when real property is sold. ¶13,283.

IMPORTANCE OF DECISIONS AND RULINGS

When you have collected and analyzed all the decisions and rulings on your problem—both those you will use and those your opponent may use—you may want to take one further step: you should find out to what extent you can use these decisions and rulings as *final* authority. In other words, you have to know to what extent the Internal Revenue Service must or will follow the principles laid down in the decisions and rulings you will cite.

This information, included in the "Interpretation of Tax Statutes" material in the "General Principles" tab of Volume 10 of P-H Federal Taxes, is illustrated below. Here is an explanation of why the Internal Revenue Service may follow a decision of a U.S. Court of Appeals in one instance, and not in another, of why the Tax Court may rule one way on a given case one time, and rule another way on a similiar case.

INTERPRETATION OF TAX STATUTES
P-H EXPLANATION

¶41,351   The fundamental rule in interpreting a statute is to get at the intention of the legislature that enacted it. Three branches of the Government furnish official sources through which to discover that intention:

(1)   legislative branch—Congressional Committee Reports;

(2)   judicial branch—court decisions;

(3)   administrative branch—Treasury Regulations and Commissioner's rulings. See ¶41,861.

(a) Congressional committee reports.—When the language of a law is not clear, congressional intent may determine judicial interpretation. This intent is frequently revealed in committee reports written in conjunction with the enactment of the law. Committee Reports reflecting enacted laws are reproduced at the appropriate places in P-H Federal Taxes and remain there until final regulations are promulgated.

Legislative history of acts prior to the adoption of the Internal Revenue Code is in Seidman's Legislative History of Federal Income Tax Laws, published by Prentice-Hall, Inc. Committee reports relating to revenue acts of this period are published in full in Part 2, CB 1939-1. Reports on codification of internal revenue laws are in CB 1939-2, p. 532-537. Various other Committee Reports are also published in the Cumulative Bulletins. See the finding list at ¶7.

[¶41,361] Weight given to Tax Court decisions.—Where the Tax Court decides in favor of the taxpayer, the law provides that the amount disallowed shall not be assessed. However, the Government has the right to file a petition for review. It is clear, therefore, that the Commissioner is not bound to follow decisions of the Tax Court, although it has done so in the majority of instances. In this connection, the weekly Internal Revenue Bulletin contains the following announcement:

It is the policy of the Internal Revenue Service to announce in the Internal Revenue Bulletin at the earliest practicable date the determination of the Commissioner to acquiesce or not to acquiesce in a decision of the Tax Court of the United States which disallows a deficiency in tax determined by the Commissioner to be due. Notice that the Commissioner has acquiesced or nonacquiesced in a decision of the Tax Court relates only to the issue or issues decided adversely to the Government. Decisions so acquiesced in should be relied upon by officers and employees of the Internal Revenue Service as precedents in the disposition of other cases. (No announcements are made in the Bulletin with respect to memorandum opinions [i.e., TC Memo decisions] of the Tax Court.)

Acquiescence by the Commissioner in a Tax Court decision usually means that the decision will be accepted by the Commissioner as a precedent in closing similar cases. However, the Commissioner has, in a few instances, revoked or withdrawn his acquiescence, and the right to do so was upheld in:

Rosen v U.S. (3 Cir;1961), 7 AFTR2d 963,

SUBSTANCE V. FORM

Hundreds of tax cases have been decided under the Supreme Court rule that substance controls, rather than form. The application of the rule is not limited to any one subject. The Commissioner may invoke it, for example, to disallow a deduction, to increase income, or to deny the existence of a particular type of taxable or nontaxable entity. And in some instances it has been relied upon successfully by taxpayers. The importance of the rule is emphasized in many Supreme Court decisions. Because of the broad scope of the rule, decisions involving it are brought together and classified in one place. See the "General Principles" tab in Volume 10 of P-H Federal Taxes.

P-H EXPLANATION

¶41,001   The rule that the substance of a transaction, rather than its mere form, controls tax liability, is one of very wide application. It can affect the amount of taxable income from practically any type of transaction. It is also applied frequently to settle questions of who is taxable on certain income. Numerous decisions of the Supreme Court [¶41,002] and hundreds of decisions of lower courts have discussed and applied the rule. It is also incorporated in several sections of the law.

Form is a pattern or scheme, the aspect under which a thing appears, as distinguished from,

Substance, that which underlies all outward manifestations—the reality itself.

However, even though the issue in a decision comes within the general principles of substance v form, it is not necessarily earmarked as such. Frequently, terms other than "substance" and "form" may be used. The following are examples:

"The question always is whether the transaction is in fact what it appears to be in form." *Chisholm v. Comm.* [¶41,015]. Taxpayer having a purpose "which defeats or contradicts the apparent transaction". *Chisholm v. Comm.,* above.

A result reached by a "devious path", which could have been reached by a "straight path", *Minnesota Tea Co. v. Helvering* [¶41,002]. "Artifice" rather than "reality". *Gregory v. Helvering* [¶41,002]. "Transactions which do not vary, control, or change the flow of economic benefits". *Higgins v. Smith* [¶41,002].

Questions of substance v. form are usually raised by the Government—not by the taxpayer. The Government usually contends that the substance of a particular transaction differs from its form, and should control tax liability. But occasionally the Government is on the other side of the argument, and contends that the taxpayer is bound by the form in which he placed the transaction, while the taxpayer tries to show that the substance differs from the form, and is controlling.

P-H EXPLANATION

¶41,002   **Supreme Court Decisions.**—The rule of substance v. form has been stated by the Supreme Court as follows:

[Excerpts supported by more than a dozen Supreme Court decisions follow.]

CHECK LISTS

Illustrated below is a page from the Check List division in Volume 1 of **FEDERAL TAXES**. These lists are prepared particularly for use in the preparation of tax returns. They have been prepared for the following topics:

Items included in gross income.

Exclusions from gross income.

Deductible items.

Nondeductible items.

Each check list includes a paragraph reference to the material in **FEDERAL TAXES** explaining the item listed.

DEDUCTIBLE ITEMS

[¶1203]   Introduction.—Check this list to be sure you have not overlooked any deductions. For a checklist of items eligible or ineligible for the investment credit see ¶5125.

Classification of deductible items for individuals.—Deductible items in general are classified into (1) those deductible from gross income to arrive at adjusted gross income and (2) those deductible from adjusted gross income as "excess itemized deductions" to arrive at taxable income. Adjusted gross income does not apply to corporations, estates and trusts.

Don't deduct a doubtful item without reading the paragraph referred to; your situation may be different. If it is, check it in the list of nondeductible items at ¶1204.

For a full explanation of adjusted gross income and its effect on tax liability of individuals, see ¶7611 et seq.

Deductions on joint return of husband and wife.—The rules applicable are explained in ¶35,073.

Special rules govern the taxation of nonresident aliens and foreign corporations and the deductions and credits to which they may be entitled. See ¶30,181 et seq.

——————————— **All references are to PARAGRAPH [¶] NUMBERS** ———————————

— A —

Abandoned property:
. assets scrapped ..14,224 et seq.; 14,251(5); 15,421
. building project ..14,249(5)
. liquidation plans ..14,249(5)
. mineral investment ..14,245
. new business enterprise (limited) ..14,078; 14,180; 14,249(15)
. trade catalogue, obsolete ..14,235(10)
Accounting fees:
. auditing constituent companies, consolidation ..16,597(25)
. business expense ..11,073
. cost accounting system ..11,074(5)
. inventory audits ..11,451(20)
. paid by investor (some) ..16,328(10)
. professional services relating to taxes ..16,355; 16,357
. real estate operator ..16,333
. system installation ..11,074(5)
Activities not engaged in for profit (limited) ..16,259

Ambulance hire (limitation) ..16,380
Amortization:
. bonds discount and issuance expense ..7349; 11,313
. child-care facilities ..16,290
. coal mine safety equipment ..16,287
. improvements by lessee ..11,851; 16,232
. intangible drilling costs (some) ..16,998
. in lieu of tax preference deductions (some) ..6116
. on-job training facilites ..16,290
. organization expenses, corporations ..16,575
. organization expenses, partnerships ..28,653
. pollution control facilities ..15,665
. premium on bonds (some) ..16,110
. production costs, films, books, etc. ..16,979
. railroad grading and tunnel bores ..16,273
. railroad rolling stock ..16,266
. real property construction period interest and taxes ..16,293
. rehabilitation expenditures for certified historic structures ..16,297
. trade-mark, foreign registration ..16,226

BOXED ITEMS IN THE INDEX

Illustrated below is an index page (Volume 1, P-H Federal Taxes) showing a boxed item on "Accounting Methods." Similiar boxed items appear throughout the index for all major topics.

This device is of particular assistance to the tax specialist who has a general problem. For example, he or she is preparing a tax return for a farmer, and wants to know all about depreciation. Rather than read through a column on references on "Accounting Methods," he or she can quickly look at the boxed item and come to the sub-head "Depreciation."

---

[3]   **ACCOUNTANTS—ACCOUNTING**   Fed. Index—**105**

———— **Boldface** references are to the Code—*Italic* references are to Regulations ————

Accountants: (continued):
. *practice before TC (continued):*
.. application form 39,243
. practice of law .... *39,820;* 39,882(20)—(30)
. privileged communications ... 38,511(15); 39,650
. records of, as evidence before TC ... 39,127.15; 39,643(1)
. records, subpoena .... 39,643(20)
. request for prompt assessment ...... 36,466(10)
. returns prepared by:
.. delinquency due to illness or death . 37,229(10)
.. disclosure of information .... *38,571.35(e);* 39,647(150)
.. false or fraudulent .... 38,548(10)
.. recompense for errors . 7226(35); 8568(25)(40)
. sale of practice .... 15,351(7); 16,724(10)
.. good will .... 32,156(20)(25)
. self-employment tax .... *34,043;* 34,082(20)
. signature requirement, return preparation .... 37,508(10)

Accounting methods (continued):
. advance payments .... 20,300; *20,301;* 20,810(15)
. affiliated group 34,359; *34,383*
.. conformance in method .... 34,359(10)
.. percentage of completion method .. 34,359(10)
. allocation of income, deductions, etc. .... 20,901—20,913
. automatic data processing 20,060; 35,496
. "(b)(1)(ii) method", credit purposes ...... 20,300; *20,301(b)(1)(ii)*
. bad debt deductions . 14,701; **14,702(a), (c), (g);** *14,706(b);* 14,844; 14,880; 14,890
.. banks: See "Banks, bad debts deduction"
. bank deposits .... 33,971—33,974
. bankruptcy .... **33,605(g)**
. banks: See "Banks, accounting methods"

〜〜〜〜〜〜〜〜〜〜〜〜〜〜〜〜〜〜〜〜〜

Accounting for collected taxes .. 39,442 et seq.

═══════════════════════════════

ACCOUNTING METHODS *See also Pilot Chart ¶ 20,000*
Major subject index; for detailed index, see items following this box.
Accrual basis 20,068
Allocation of income, deductions, etc. 20,901—20,913
Automatic data processing 20,060; 35,496
Bad debts .... *14,706(b);* **14,844; 14,880**
Cash bases 20,067
Change of method .... 20,081—20,114
Depletion .... 22,316(b)
Depreciation .... 17,343(c)(4); 17,371
Earnings and profits .... 17,343(c)(4); 17,371
Farmers 7165; 20,736
Hybrid system 20,069
Installment sales .... 20,464—20,466
Long-term contracts .... 20,260—20,276
Prepaid income .... 20,305 et seq.
Reflection of income .... 20,060—20,066

Accounting methods .... 20,060 et seq.
See also "Books and records"
. accounting practice distinguished ..... 20,083(7)
. accrual: See "Accrual basis of accounting"
. adequacy .... **20,061(b);** *20,062(b);* 33,956
. adjustments:
.. change in method .... 20,801—20,815
.. returned merchandise 20,548; **20,548.5;** *20,548.16*

... "positive adjustments" 20,083
.. affiliated corporations .... 34,359(10)
.. agreement as to allocation method *20,808*
.. allocation of adjustments differing from prescribed method *20,808*
... returned merchandise, publishers and distributors 20,548; **20,548.5**
.. amended returns .... 20,082(5)—(15)
.. application .... *14,706(b); 18,515(d)(2); 20,062(e);* 20,081; 20,082(5)(6)(25); *20,083(7);* 20,775
.. assessment of deficiency .... **20,802(b)(3);** *20,805(c); 20,807; 20,809;* 20,810(25)
.. assets placed in service, cost basis .. 20,810(5)
.. bad debts: See "Bad debts, change in accounting method"
.. baseball player contracts .... 20,810(5)
.. blocked foreign income .... 20,293; 20,906(30)
.. bonuses, time for deduction as ...... 20,810(5)
.. capital loss carryovers . **20,802(b)(3);** *20,805(c)*
.. class life system 15,466.1
.. C.O.D. sales .... 20,068(50)
.. Commissioner's consent . **20,061(e);** *20,062(e);* 20,081—20,085; 20,571(5)
.. Commissioner's direction ..... *20,062(c)(2);* 20,081—20,085; 20,810(5)(10)
.. Commissioner's power to require 20,087
.. Commodity Credit loans *7898*
.. completed contract to percentage of completion .... 20,083(5)
.. computation of taxable income ...... 20,083(7)
.. conference in National Office .... 20,083(7)
.. consent to adjustments *20,808*
.. consolidated returns .... *34,383(b);* 34,351; 34,359(10)
.. constant cost to lower of cost or market .... 20,810(5)

〜〜〜〜〜〜〜〜〜〜〜〜〜〜〜〜〜〜〜〜〜

TAX ELECTIONS CHECKLIST

The checklist of tax elections is designed to draw a tax planner or preparer's attention to the various tax choices offered by the tax laws. The checklist, arranged in the numerical Code section order, specifies the nature of the election, the time by which the election must be made under the law or Regulations and the manner in which it's made. The entries that list the type or nature of the election also refer you to the paragraph [¶] in the P-H Federal Taxes Service which explains the election and provides further details. "Annual" elections are those made only for a given tax year.

Whenever the checklist says that an election must be made by the "due date of the return", it means the filing date including extensions unless stated otherwise. Elections that have to be made "within the limitation period" are usually made on a return (or amended return) within the period of limitation for filing a claim for credit or refund prescribed by Sec. 6511(a), (generally 3 years from the time the return is filed or 2 years from the time the tax is paid). An election that has to be made with the return for the "first year covered" must be made with the return for the first year to which the election is to apply. Public Laws (P.L.) cited in the checklist are in the Amending Acts tab.

Code Sec.	Nature of Election	Must be Made by	How Made
37(e)(2)	Credit for elderly... age 65 or older... income from public retirement systems (annual). ¶4081.	Within limitations period.	On Form 1040.
44B	Targeted jobs credit for newly hired employees (annual) ¶4216.	Within 3 years after due date of return excluding extensions.	Claim credit on return.
44F(e)(4)	Research & experimental expense credit ... treatment as qualified fund (annual). ¶4271.	Within limitations period.	Form 6765 with return.
46(a)(2)(E), 48(n)	Investment credit ... employee plan percentage ... pre-1983 rules (annual). ¶5156.	By due date of return.	Statement with return.
46(d)	Investment credit ... construction of Sec. 38 property ... qualified progress expenditures. ¶5053.	With return for first year covered.	Statement with original return.
48(d)	Investment credit ... leased property ... lessor's pass-through to lessee (annual) ¶5144.	By due date of lessee's return for year possession transferred.	Statement with lessee.
48(q)(4)	Investment credit ... property placed in service after 1982 ... reduced credit in lieu of basis adjustment ¶15,001.	With return for year property placed in service.	Statement with return.
57(c)(2)	Net lease ... Tax preference item for minimum tax ... treatment of multiple leases as a single lease for 15% test (annual). ¶13,001(i)(5).	By due date of return.	Statement with return.

FEDERAL TAX RATE TABLES AND CHARTS

If the information you are seeking is merely a certain rate of tax, use the Tax Tables and Charts in Volume 1 of **P-H FEDERAL TAXES**; tab 3100 for present rates. Rates under prior law are in Volume 10, under the Prior Law tab (45,000) at ¶45,901 et seq. Charts for prior rates go back to 1909.

PRESENT LAW TAX TABLES

WEEKLY PAYROLL PERIOD — MARRIED PERSONS

Wages: $0—$409.99   (For Wages Paid After June 1983 and Before January 1985)

WEEKLY MARRIED PERSONS

At least	But less than	0	1	2	3	4	5	6	7	8	9	10
$0	$47											
47	48	.20										
48	49	.30										
49	50	.40										
50	51	.50										
51	52	.60										
52	53	.80										
53	54	.90										
54	55	1.00										
55	56	1.10										
56	57	1.20										
57	58	1.40										
58	59	1.50										
59	60	1.60										
60	62	1.80										
62	64	2.00										
64	66	2.30										
66	68	2.50	.20									
68	70	2.70	.40									
70	72	3.00	.70									
72	74	3.20	.90									
74	76	3.50	1.20									
76	78	3.70	1.40									
78	80	3.90	1.60									
80	82	4.20	1.90									
82	84	4.40	2.10									
84	86	4.70	2.40									
86	88	4.90	2.60	.30								
88	90	5.10	2.80	.50								
90	92	5.40	3.10	.80								
92	94	5.60	3.30	1.00								
94	96	5.90	3.60	1.20								
96	98	6.10	3.80	1.50								
98	100	6.30	4.00	1.70								
100	105	6.80	4.50	2.10								
At least	But less than	0	1	2	3	4	5	6	7	8	9	10
105	110	7.40	5.10	2.70	.40							
110	115	8.00	5.70	3.30	1.00							
115	120	8.60	6.30	3.90	1.60							
120	125	9.20	6.90	4.50	2.20							
125	130	9.80	7.50	5.10	2.80	.50						
130	135	10.40	8.10	5.70	3.40	1.10						
135	140	11.00	8.70	6.30	4.00	1.70						
140	145	11.60	9.30	6.90	4.60	2.30						
145	150	12.20	9.90	7.50	5.20	2.90	.60					
150	160	13.10	10.80	8.40	6.10	3.80	1.50					
160	170	14.30	12.00	9.60	7.30	5.00	2.70	.40				
170	180	15.50	13.20	10.80	8.50	6.20	3.90	1.60				
180	190	16.70	14.40	12.00	9.70	7.40	5.10	2.80	.50			
190	200	18.40	15.60	13.20	10.90	8.60	6.30	4.00	1.70			
200	210	20.10	16.80	14.40	12.10	9.80	7.50	5.20	2.90	.60		
210	220	21.80	18.50	15.60	13.30	11.00	8.70	6.40	4.10	1.80		
220	230	23.50	20.20	16.90	14.50	12.20	9.90	7.60	5.30	3.00	.70	
230	240	25.20	21.90	18.60	15.70	13.40	11.10	8.80	6.50	4.20	1.90	
240	250	26.90	23.60	20.30	17.10	14.60	12.30	10.00	7.70	5.40	3.10	.80
250	260	28.60	25.30	22.00	18.80	15.80	13.50	11.20	8.90	6.60	4.30	2.00
260	270	30.30	27.00	23.70	20.50	17.20	14.70	12.40	10.10	7.80	5.50	3.20
270	280	32.00	28.70	25.40	22.20	18.90	15.90	13.60	11.30	9.00	6.70	4.40
280	290	33.70	30.40	27.10	23.90	20.60	17.30	14.80	12.50	10.20	7.90	5.60
290	300	35.40	32.10	28.80	25.60	22.30	19.00	16.00	13.70	11.40	9.10	6.80
300	310	37.10	33.80	30.50	27.30	24.00	20.70	17.50	14.90	12.60	10.30	8.00

INDEX TO TAX ARTICLES

The Index To Tax Articles (Volume 1, P-H Federal Taxes) lists tax articles appearing in other publications (law journals, magazines, etc.) to supplement your research. The table provides the name of the publication, and the volume and page number where each article appears. Abbreviations follow *A Uniform System of Citation* (12th edition), published by the Harvard Law Review Association. If you don't have an article you want, you may order it from the publisher listed at ¶3051.

How to use this table.—The tax articles are listed under the same paragraph numbers used in P-H Federal Taxes. First, research your subject in P-H Federal Taxes. Then check the table for the same paragraph numbers. They will list tax articles on the same subject, to supplement your research.

Example.—If you have read ¶33,361 in P-H Federal Taxes on Subchapter S (Sec. 1371 et seq.) corporations, find ¶33,361 in the table. It lists tax articles written on the same subject.

P-H Publications.—The symbol ( ) indicates a reference to tax articles appearing in P-H "Tax Ideas," P-H "Tax Exempt Organizations," P-H "U.S. Taxation of International Operations," P-H "Oil and Gas/Natural Resources Taxes," P-H "Successful Estate Planning Ideas and Methods" or P-H "Wills-Trusts Estate Planning Forms." These articles provide additional editorial analysis and tax-saving ideas.

S Corporations

33,347... "A Walking Tour Through S-Land" by Joel E. Miller, 10 J. Real Estate Tax. 235 (Spring 1983)

"An Analysis of the Subchapter S Revision Act: Eligibility, Election, Termination" by Richard A. Shaw and Jerald D. August, 58 J. Taxation 2 (Jan. 1983)

"New S Corporation Rules Revised and Explained by Technical Corrections Act, Temporary Regs." by Fred B. Weil and Robert W. Wood, 11 Taxation for Lawyers 272 (March/April; 1983) and 30 Taxation for Accountants 142 (March 1983)

"Opportunities and Problems With Sub S Holdings of Estates and Trusts" by John B. Huffaker and Albert L. Doering, III, 58 J. Taxation 130 (March 1983)

"Subchapter S Corporations Made Simpler by New Law, but not all Changes are Improvements" by Fred B. Weil and Robert W. Wood, 11 Taxation for Lawyers 196 (Jan./Feb. 1983) and 29 Taxation for Accountants 348 (Dec. 1982)

"Subchapter S Revision Act: Distributions, Taxable Years and Other Changes" by Richard A. Shaw and Jerald D. August, 58 J. Taxation 300 (May 1983)

"Subchapter S Revision Act Makes Significant Changes in Taxing S Corporation Operations" by Richard A. Shaw and Jerald D. August, 58 J. Taxation 84 (Feb. 1983)

"Taxing Corporate Acquisitions" by Martin D. Ginsburg, 38 Tax L. Rev. 171 (Winter 1983)

"The Subchapter S Revision Act of 1982 (Part I)" by Lorence L. Bravenec, 14 Tax Adviser 194 (Apr. 1983), (Part II) 14 Tax Adviser 280 (May 1983)

The following flow charts of RESEARCH IN FEDERAL TAXATION provide a bird's-eye view of how to research using the P-H FEDERAL TAXES SERVICE.

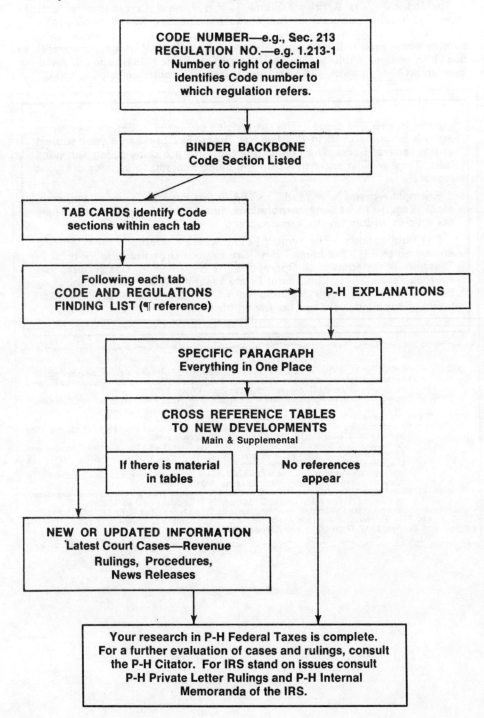

RESEARCHING "KEY WORD"
USING INDEX AND BINDER BACKBONE APPROACH

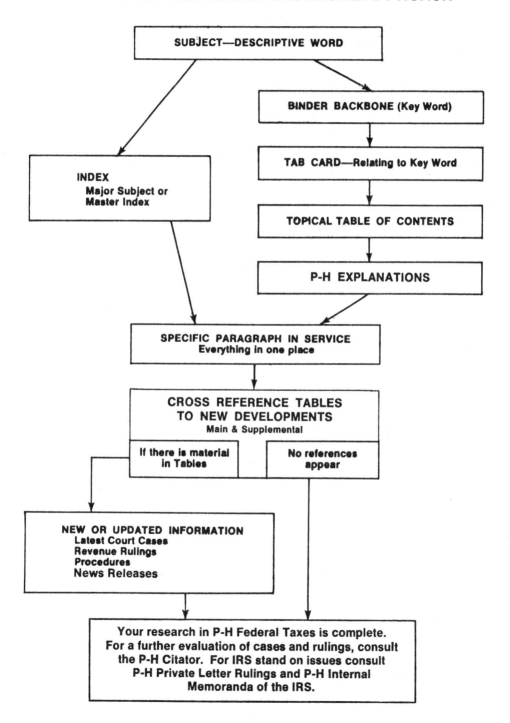

RESEARCH
USING RULINGS

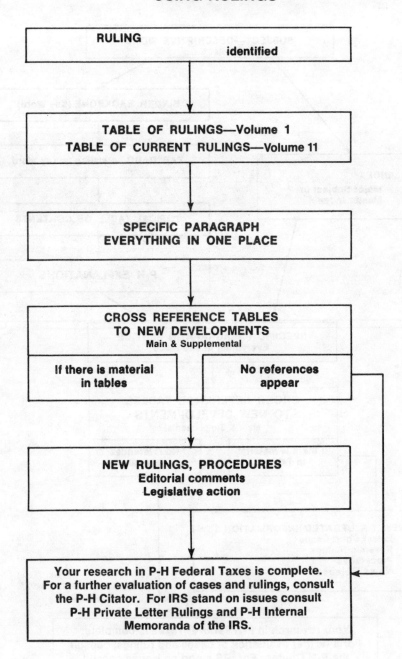

RULING
identified

TABLE OF RULINGS—Volume 1
TABLE OF CURRENT RULINGS—Volume 11

SPECIFIC PARAGRAPH
EVERYTHING IN ONE PLACE

CROSS REFERENCE TABLES
TO NEW DEVELOPMENTS
Main & Supplemental

If there is material
in tables

No references
appear

NEW RULINGS, PROCEDURES
Editorial comments
Legislative action

Your research in P-H Federal Taxes is complete.
For a further evaluation of cases and rulings, consult
the P-H Citator. For IRS stand on issues consult
P-H Private Letter Rulings and P-H Internal
Memoranda of the IRS.

RESEARCH
USING CASE NAME

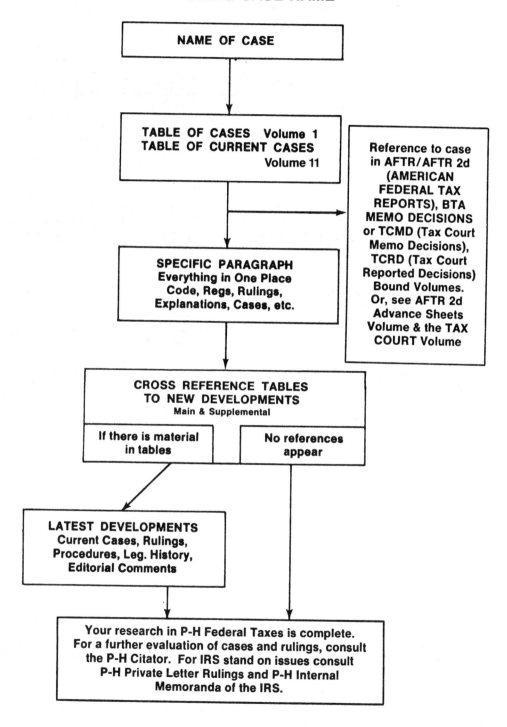

NAME OF CASE

TABLE OF CASES   Volume 1
TABLE OF CURRENT CASES
                                    Volume 11

Reference to case
in AFTR/AFTR 2d
(AMERICAN
FEDERAL TAX
REPORTS), BTA
MEMO DECISIONS
or TCMD (Tax Court
Memo Decisions),
TCRD (Tax Court
Reported Decisions)
Bound Volumes.
Or, see AFTR 2d
Advance Sheets
Volume & the TAX
COURT Volume

SPECIFIC PARAGRAPH
Everything in One Place
Code, Regs, Rulings,
Explanations, Cases, etc.

CROSS REFERENCE TABLES
TO NEW DEVELOPMENTS
Main & Supplemental

If there is material
in tables

No references
appear

LATEST DEVELOPMENTS
Current Cases, Rulings,
Procedures, Leg. History,
Editorial Comments

Your research in P-H Federal Taxes is complete.
For a further evaluation of cases and rulings, consult
the P-H Citator. For IRS stand on issues consult
P-H Private Letter Rulings and P-H Internal
Memoranda of the IRS.

PART V
PHINet

Stamped with our new logotype, PHINet is the official trademark of "Prentice-Hall Information Network," a special project within our Information Services Division—a team devoted to converting any number of our editorially rich, traditionally print "databases" into high-speed electronic access-and-delivery systems. We're introducing the first PHINet service—the Prentice-Hall FedTax Database Service, a computerized, online research-and-retrieval system created especially for tax practitioners as a professional tax-planning tool. From the day it's a "go," Prentice-Hall's 10-volume Federal Taxes Looseleaf Services can be *immediately accessed* and *selectively retrieved* by any subscriber hooked into the new PHINet time-sharing network.

What's in the FedTax Database: Specifically, the PHINet user can tap our online FedTax Database for accurate information in any of these areas:

- *Developments and trends:* Explanatory updates, commentary, and analysis researched and written by the Prentice-Hall Information Services Division's top-flight editorial staff
- *Internal Revenue Code:* Full text of the 1954 Internal Revenue Code, as amended, which can be retrieved by Code section
- *Committee reports:* Full text of reports from legislative committees (House Ways and Means, Senate, Finance, Conference Committees)
- *Regulations:* Full text of final, proposed, and temporary Treasury regulations
- *Revenue procedures:* Full text of Internal Revenue Service procedural guidelines
- *Annotations:* Abstracts or digests of cases and rulings, as related to specific Code sections

In early 1984, our plans call for also "bringing up" on the PHINet FedTax Database these critical documents:

- *American Federal Tax Reports,* AFTR 2d Series, Vols. 39-51 (full text from 1977 to date)
- *Tax Court Memo Decisions,* Vols. 46-51 (full text from 1977 to date)

Getting into the FedTax Database: Just how does one get *into* this storehouse—and find precisely what's needed? Through PHINet's fast, flexible, easy-to-use search system. Following a simple command procedure (based on standard tax research methods), any PHINet user can search the FedTax Database by *keyword* or *phrase,* by *Code section* or *case name,* and through numerous other ways not possible with the print service—expanding or limiting the search as necessary. The PHINet user also "commands" the *level of detail* delivered by the search request: all the material, certain types of materials, or simply references only.

Within seconds after the search-query command is entered into the PHINet system (through a wide variety of terminals, as well as microcomputers), the FedTax Database has been completely searched for every possible pertinent reference—and the results are flashed on the user's video screen. Because the FedTax Database is *itself* so comprehensive and the computer search is totally *thorough,* the PHINet user can be confident that *every* relevant item requested by the search has been captured and brought up.

And that's the essence of our first PHINet—Prentice-Hall's own comprehensive federal tax information storehouse *linked to* a dynamic new technology, bringing tax research up to an incomparable level of speed and accuracy.

PHINet's ongoing research has already identified how effectively the FedTax Database Service speeds up and eases a variety of tax-research tasks—specifically because the database *includes* Prentice-Hall's distinguished editorial analyses and interpretive coverage of developing issues. The PHINet system, from the feedback we've monitored, promises much-needed speed and accuracy in all these research assignments:

- Isolating a quick "answer" to a very specific "question"
- Developing an overview (initial or "refresher") of a special tax area
- Charting an efficient direction into an area that may be somewhat unfamiliar to the practitioner
- Monitoring "priority" issues on an ongoing basis, or, perhaps most important,
- Gathering support for a particular position.

The Complete Federal Tax Library...

P-H
INFORMATION
SERVICES
DIVISION